Classical Greece

A Captivating Guide to an Era in Ancient Greece That Strongly Influenced Western Civilization, Starting from the Persian Wars and Rise of Athens to the Death of Alexander the Great

© Copyright 2021

All Rights Reserved. No part of this book may be reproduced in any form without permission in writing from the author. Reviewers may quote brief passages in reviews.

Disclaimer: No part of this publication may be reproduced or transmitted in any form or by any means, mechanical or electronic, including photocopying or recording, or by any information storage and retrieval system, or transmitted by email without permission in writing from the publisher.

While all attempts have been made to verify the information provided in this publication, neither the author nor the publisher assumes any responsibility for errors, omissions or contrary interpretations of the subject matter herein.

This book is for entertainment purposes only. The views expressed are those of the author alone, and should not be taken as expert instruction or commands. The reader is responsible for his or her own actions.

Adherence to all applicable laws and regulations, including international, federal, state and local laws governing professional licensing, business practices, advertising and all other aspects of doing business in the US, Canada, UK or any other jurisdiction is the sole responsibility of the purchaser or reader.

Neither the author nor the publisher assumes any responsibility or liability whatsoever on the behalf of the purchaser or reader of these materials. Any perceived slight of any individual or organization is purely unintentional.

Free Bonus from Captivating History (Available for a Limited time)

Hi History Lovers!

Now you have a chance to join our exclusive history list so you can get your first history ebook for free as well as discounts and a potential to get more history books for free! Simply visit the link below to join.

Captivatinghistory.com/ebook

Also, make sure to follow us on Facebook, Twitter and Youtube by searching for Captivating History.

Contents

INTRODUCTION 1
CHAPTER 1: PRELUDE TO THE CLASSICAL PERIOD 4
CHAPTER 2: OLIGARCHY, TYRANNY, AND DEMOCRACY 16
CHAPTER 3: THE PERSIAN WARS (499-449 BCE) 32
CHAPTER 4: THE RISE OF ATHENS AND THE DELIAN LEAGUE 40
CHAPTER 5: CULTURE AND SOCIETY OF CLASSICAL ATHENS 50
CHAPTER 6: THE PELOPONNESIAN WAR 61
CHAPTER 7: THE RISE OF MACEDON 75
CHAPTER 8: ALEXANDER THE GREAT 85
CONCLUSION 96
HERE'S ANOTHER BOOK BY CAPTIVATING HISTORY THAT YOU MIGHT LIKE 99
FREE BONUS FROM CAPTIVATING HISTORY (AVAILABLE FOR A LIMITED TIME) 100
REFERENCES 101

Introduction

The period of Greek history between 478 and 323 is what we now refer to as classical Greece. This was the period when the concept of democracy first appeared. Democracy was the response to the events that occurred during the Archaic period, and it brought new thought to how a state should be governed and how the people should behave. Tyrants were then brought down, and a new structure of polis was promoted, with the people making the majority of the political and social decisions. But this didn't come easily, and various cities developed their own democracies in different ways. Athens rose as the culturally dominant state; thus, most evidence we have on this period comes from Athens. This is why it is easiest to concentrate on the events that involved this particular Greek polis.

After the Persian Wars, Sparta withdrew to the Peloponnese while Athens started an alliance known as the Delian League to continue the struggle against Persia. Through this league, Athens became the most powerful and the richest polis of mainland Greece, and it sought to exploit this advantage. All other cities transformed from being equal members of the Delian League into being subjects of Athens, and the period of the Athenian empire began. It wasn't an empire in the modern sense of the word. In fact, it didn't even consider itself an empire. But in an imperialistic manner, Athens imposed itself on others, and soon enough, it became clear that Athens made all the decisions and collected the revenues of all the other member city-states of the Delian league. Athens had shifted the power balance to its advantage, forcing Sparta to respond. The result was the Peloponnesian War (431-404), in which Sparta tried to break Athens's powerful grip on the Greek world. The result was the decline of Athens's power, but Sparta managed to achieve its goals by bringing Persia back into Greek affairs.

Although utterly defeated, Athens made a remarkable recovery and was able to join Sparta and Thebes in a power struggle that lasted for forty years after the end of the Peloponnesian War. Many alliances were created and broken during this period, and Persia continued to meddle in Greek politics until it finally regained the Anatolian Greek poleis in 387/6 BCE. Sparta was defeated in 371 by Thebes, and although it tried, it never again managed to return to its former glory. The Persians planned to integrate all of Greece into its powerful empire, and they knew very well that there was no Greek military commander able to oppose them.

But in the north, the Kingdom of Macedonia rose to power under the leadership of King Philip II. The Greeks took the opportunity to defend themselves and united again against their common enemy: Persia. By 336, Philip II had managed to create the Corinthian League and drive out the Persians. He planned to continue his efforts by conquering all of his enemy's territories, but his dream was cut short by an assassin. His son, Alexander the Great, continued Philip's plans, and he conquered the whole known world.

The Persians, who wanted Greece to become part of their empire, now found themselves as an extension of the Greek world. But the death of Alexander the Great brought an end to his vast empire, which ended up being divided between four of his most powerful generals. The new kingdoms that sprouted from the territories Alexander controlled transformed the world with new political, cultural, and social ideas. A new era began, one that modern scholars named the Hellenistic age.

Although the events of classical Greece are undoubtedly interesting, this was a period of great social and cultural changes too. The development of the polis, democracy, and citizenship, as well as the rise of tragedy and comedy, gave the people a voice on contemporary issues. In tragedies and comedies, these issues were often voiced by women. This was impossible in reality, as women had no political rights, but it was possible in an imaginary world. Women, the silent foundation of Greek society, transformed into brave heroines who were able to influence events and make their own independent decisions in the plays of great literary men such as Sophocles and Aristophanes.

Plays, like anything else in classical Greece, were interwoven with religion and the worship of the gods on Mount Olympus. Religion dictated the citizens' behavior since one's fortune depended on his actions and whether they pleased or displeased the divine. Religion was one of the many aspects of state life, and priests often took state offices. The temples and the many religious ceremonies and festivals were regulated and financed by the state or by wealthy state officials. But the religion itself wasn't simply a set of correct beliefs. It was more about the rituals and their correct performance, one on which the whole community's future depended. It was through religious festivals that the people pleased the gods, and rituals also included athletic and playwriting competitions. Culture, public life, politics, and religion were all parts that made up a single individual, a citizen of a polis set in classical Greece.

Chapter 1: Prelude to the Classical Period

Map of Greece, drawn in 1791
https://en.wikipedia.org/wiki/Classical_Greece#/media/File:Map_of_Greece,_Archipelago_and_part_of_Anadoli;_Louis_Stanislas_d'Arcy_Delarochette_1791.jpg

The Dark Ages

In the period between 1200 and 1000 BCE, the Greek world was suffering the downfall of the Mycenaean civilization. The economic crash, local conflicts, and the movement of the people that followed the Myceneans' fall are staples of what is known as the Greek Dark Ages. Whole kingdoms and independent cities of the Near East were obliterated, which resulted in a weak economy and grinding poverty to the Greek population that depended on trade. But there is a veil of mystery covering this period because not much written evidence survived. And it is the very absence of written sources from the Greek world that testifies to the gruesomeness of the period. It is both the general poverty of the people and the lack of evidence of this period that prompted modern historians to name it the "Dark Ages."

The Near East ended its Dark Ages before Greece. There, the people managed to recover their economy and politics by 900 BCE, while in Greece, the end of the Dark Ages came 150 years later, in the mid-8th century BCE. Although the recovery was slow in Greece, the survivors of the Mycenaean civilization never really lost their contact with the Near East. Trade, technology, religious traditions, and ideas could flow freely. Thus, during this period, the Greeks set the foundations for the values, traditions, and the new forms of social and political systems that would come into full life during the Archaic and Classical periods.

The Greek Dark Ages started with the loss of technology and the ability to write. Although this loss was never complete, it happened due to the economic crisis that came when the Mycenaean economic system fell after prolonged periods of war. The Mycenaean script was extremely difficult to learn, and it remained in use only among court scribes. With the downfall of civilization, the remaining Greek society lost the need for scribes. Since they didn't have an economy, there was no demand for recordings of the flow of goods and money. However, the lack of a written language allowed the oral tradition to survive and prosper. Storytelling, music, poetry, and other oral performances survived, and they transmitted the cultural ideas of the Greeks as an ethnic group from generation to generation. But as modern history discovered, the Greek oral tradition wasn't always true. For example, tradition says that Dorians invaded mainland Greece and settled there, eventually becoming the Spartans. There are no written records or archaeological findings that can support this claim. It seems that there was never really any Dorian invasion.

The archaeological findings that are dated to 900 BCE show that this was a period when people of mainland Greece started recovering their wealth. They started using luxurious items in burial ceremonies, and many people were buried with expensive goods. But the economic recovery isn't the only thing that is evident from these findings. It seems that a social hierarchy was starting to spread through Greece, as only some people were wealthy while the majority were poor. In the earlier stages of the Greek Dark Ages, most of the findings indicate people could not afford luxurious grave offerings; all that was found in burial sites were clay pots. But after 900 BCE, the trade and the economy started developing, and items such as iron weapons, jewelry, and cutlery could be found in graves. Since they were all made out of iron, it is evident that around 900 BCE, the Greeks imported the technology and knowledge of how to produce it from the Near East.

The use of iron expanded to agriculture. Because it was easier to procure and work with, it also became a cheaper option than bronze. The production of food increased with the introduction of iron tools, and the population started booming. Greek agriculture started recovering by 850 BCE, with the expansion of the grain fields and the livestock herds. The population growth was only natural, and this repopulation created a Greek society ready to invent new political forms and slowly move into democracy.

The elite existed by this time, and they were the wealthiest of the Greeks. However, they were never an aristocracy in the modern Western sense. The term aristocracy comes from the Greek language, and it means "the rule of the best," or what we would know as nobility. But Greeks never had official nobility, such as the aristocrats of western European countries, who inherited their status by being born into an aristocratic family. In the Greek sense, it is better to use the term "elite," as anyone could rise to this social status by acquiring wealth and political power. The Greek elites were still considered the best, and they were the leaders and rulers.

This hierarchical society started developing its own moral values, which later turned into political ideals. Proper behavior within the community became paramount for the ruling elite, as they were expected to assert control over the people. The social values of the Greek Dark Ages are described in the great literary works of the *Iliad* and *Odyssey*, both dated to the middle of the 8th century BCE. The deeds and values of great Greek heroes were described in these lengthy poems, and they were considered to be the ideals to which all members of Greek society should strive. Warriors and family life were cherished, and attributes such as courage, exceptional skills, curiosity, and the tendency to raise children were values the ancient Greeks held in high regard. But the elite members of society also had to strive to achieve *arete*, a Greek word with many meanings, usually translated as "excellence." The shame of failing to achieve excellence in whatever one was doing was a constant threat for the elite. Excellence was also a moral value, and as such, it carried a strong notion of obligation and responsibility.

There was no greater place to exercise Greek values and to display the excellence one achieved than to compete in the Olympic Games. They were founded at the end of the Greek Dark Ages in 776 BCE and were held every four years within a large sanctuary in Olympia, which was dedicated to Zeus. The men who had the time and the ability to reach excellence in athletic disciplines competed in different events, such as running, wrestling, jumping, horse-riding, and many more. There were no teams, and each individual competed for himself, not as a representative of a nation or a city. The winners would receive public recognition as the best of all other male competitors, which in itself was the Greek ideal of masculine identity. Women didn't compete in the Olympic Games, but they had their own competitions in honor of Hera. Unfortunately, little is known about the competition for women, but racing was certainly one of the games.

The Development of the Polis

During the Archaic period, the Greeks developed their city-states, their most influential political entities. But the social development of Greek society started much earlier during the Greek Dark Ages (1100-750 BCE). During the Archaic period (750-500 BCE), it only culminated and developed into the form of city-states (singular: polis; plural: poleis). The population of the poleis consisted of males, females, children, slaves, and resident foreigners. However, only the males who were born in the territory of a given city-state could obtain citizenship, which would give them a set of privileges (such as the right to vote). The polis was a complex social structure with people of different origins, backgrounds, and legal and social statuses. Personal freedom was extremely important, as the poor but free people were eligible to obtain citizenship. They may have been deprived of basic necessities, but poor free men had the right to engage in political life. This was what separated them from slaves and the foreigners and what gave their lives extra meaning.

Polis is a Greek term from which the modern word "politics" is derived. It means "the city," although it is translated as city-state because, unlike modern cities, the poleis were separate political entities. Poleis didn't include only a distinct urban center protected by city walls. The surrounding countryside and the neighboring villages were also a part of the poleis. Thus, the population of one polis could include the inhabitants of the urban environment as well as the farmers and villagers scattered throughout its rural territories. The partnership that developed between various inhabitants of a polis gave the polis its distinct political characteristic. Only adult men, holders of citizenship, were allowed to participate in political life. Women and children still counted as a part of the community, and they had their legal, social, and religious parts to play.

Each polis had a patron god that was considered the city's protector and patron. For example, Athens had the goddess Athena as its city protector. That doesn't mean that each city was obliged to choose a different deity as its patron. Syracuse, for example, had the goddess Athena as their patron as well. Thebes and Delphi shared Apollo as their patron god.

The patron gods were called poliad due to their special connection to the city. However, that doesn't mean a polis didn't worship any other god. They respected and built temples to many gods in the Greek pantheon, but the poliad had a special place, and its temple would be the largest one, occupying the acropolis. The acropolis itself was the nucleus of a polis. It was a citadel, often built on elevated grounds so it could serve as a defensive structure.

Religion played a huge part in the life of ancient Greece. There were many religious festivals organized within the polis, and they were paid for by the citizens. During these festivals, animals would be sacrificed to pay respect to the many Greek gods and goddesses. Dedicated individuals, priests, and priestesses were the religious leaders of the community, and they oversaw and participated in these religious rituals.

A polis maintained relationships with its neighbors, but it was a completely independent and separate political entity. Its urban and rural citizens were tied by political unity. And while Middle Eastern traders brought artistic influences to Greece, it is unlikely they also brought their politics. This is why it is widely believed that Greece is the cradle of its political system. The city-states were organized similarly to Middle Eastern ancient city-kingdoms because the two people had reached a similar level of civilization, not because of political interference.

However, the similarity between city-states ends with the political unity of a polis. A polis's political core was different from one to another. Each city-state developed at its own pace and followed its own natural course. When the Mycenaean politics of the Greek Dark Ages went away, it left a power vacuum behind. This vacuum wasn't filled by the imperial states (like it would in the Middle East). Instead, it allowed each city to develop independently, and the larger ones never displayed a tendency to absorb the smaller cities.

Citizenship was the center of political life in the polis, as it granted the people political autonomy. We already mentioned that only adult males could be the holders of citizenship, and they could pass it to their male offspring. Women had no political autonomy, nor did children or slaves. But that doesn't mean politics didn't concern them. There were sets of laws that regulated the roles of women, children, foreigners, and slaves in society, and they had different levels of freedom attached to them. When it came to women, for instance, some laws regulated their sexual behavior and the control of property.

Citizenship meant equality before the law, and this equality never relied on the wealth of an individual. Social differentiation between the rich and poor was pronounced in the ancient Near East and in Greece during the Dark Ages. But with the development of poleis and citizenship, legal equality emerged. The poor people had a lower quality of life, and they often lacked the basic means of survival, but they were equally involved in making political decisions. Social and economic differences in Greek society still existed, and the people were divided between the elites and the commoners. It is important to make a difference between political and legal equality. Elite families had more political freedoms but were responsible for their deeds as much as any commoner.

The poleis and citizenship weren't the only political forms in place during the eight centuries of its existence (from 750 BCE until the emergence of the Roman Empire). The Greeks also knew political organizations such as federations and leagues. These organizations would politically bind, albeit loosely, a broad territory or multiple poleis into an association. However, the polis remained the nucleus of broader Greek politics.

The development of poleis in Greece wasn't an accident. The ancient Greek philosopher Aristotle observed that the emergence of the polis was only natural, as humans are social beings who tend to group around common interests. However, in Greece, geography also influenced the development of the city-states. The Greek mainland is a very mountainous area, and the cities were separated from each other by a physical barrier. Communication between the cities was hard to maintain, and it is no wonder they started developing political independence, despite the fact that they shared the same language and culture. Some city-states managed to develop independently, even though there was no physical barrier between them, such as the poleis in the plains of Boeotia. Even a single island could hold several city-states that were completely independent of each other (e.g., Lesbos had five poleis). Independence in these cases was possible because no polis controlled more land than it needed to feed its population. This is why the city-states maintained a population from several hundred up to several thousand. Athens was the biggest known polis, amounting to forty thousand people. However, Athens was able to feed its people not because it controlled a large amount of arable land but because it developed a system of food imports from abroad.

As soon as a polis grew above the number of people its arable land could support, the Greeks would migrate. The first migration started as early as the 9th century BCE with the settlement in Ionia. In 750 BCE, the Greeks started spreading from the mainland in all directions. In only two centuries, Greeks started colonies in present-day France, Spain, Sicily, South Italy, North Africa, and along the coast of the Black Sea to western Anatolia and eastern Syria. This is what scholars refer to as the Greek world. By the end of the 4th century BCE, Greece had over 1,100 small states, and it counted over

8 million people. They all shared the Greek culture and language but with localized variations.

The lack of arable land wasn't the only reason Greeks emigrated. They also started developing (or better yet reviving) the international trade in the Mediterranean, and many of them felt compelled to leave their homeland. Commercial interests urged some individuals to take up residency in far-away lands and start their own trading posts. Those who were rich enough to risk their finances would often engage in risky expeditions in search of metals. Sometimes a polis would organize these expeditions and choose one individual who would be a founder (*ktistes*) of a colony. Although the colony would develop independently from the "mother polis" (metropolis; from Greek root meter, meaning "mother"), it was expected to keep close ties. The metropolis and its colony would act as allies in times of war. But there were instances when a colony would break off from its metropolis and side with the enemy. In that case, the colony was regarded as disloyal.

Women's Rights, Marriage, and the Household

Since only adult men had the right to obtain citizenship, equality in ancient Greece was incomplete. There is an ancient Greek feminine term for a citizen, *politis*, but it bears no political significance, unlike its male counterpart, *polites*. The Greeks did refer to women as "female citizens" but only in regards to certain religious roles and to legal guardianship over women. But unlike slaves, women did have their own identity and social status. This alone secured them certain rights that the foreigners (*metics*) and slaves could not have. Free women were legally protected from being kidnapped and sold into slavery. They also had access to courts and could enter property or any other legal dispute, but they could never represent themselves. They needed a male guardian, a representative, who would speak in her name. This requirement of a male guardian speaks of the legal inequality ancient Greek women had to endure.

Every woman had a legal male guardian known as a *kyrios*. It could be her father, brother, husband, or any other man whose duty was to protect her both legally and physically. The interests of a woman were also defined by men, and it was the men who regulated women's everyday lives. Thus, women had no right to participate in politics. They were forbidden from attending political assemblies, voting, and making any political decisions.

But where women excelled was religion. They had their own female cults and could be initiated into the priesthood of certain deities just like men. The female cults were equally respected as the male ones, and they usually centered around the worship of Demeter, a goddess who promised protection from evil and peace in the afterlife. The ancient Greeks were very religious, and the Eleusinian Mysteries, an initiation ceremony of the Demeter/Persephone cult, was a sacred event. It was also a secret event, and its importance is displayed in the fact that those who revealed the rite's secrets were punished by death.

The women's responsibility was the household, which was greatly expanded with the introduction of slavery. Rich women had bigger households and more work since they had more slaves. But when it came to family life, the husband and wife were seen as partners. While men were outside farming, working, and participating in politics, the women's place was inside, managing a household. Roman women held a similar status during the later Roman Empire.

The modern word "economy" comes from the Greek word for household (*oikonomia*). Women were expected to raise children, prepare or supervise food preparation and preservation, keep accounts of the family's finances, make clothing, manage the slaves, and nurse their family members and slaves when they were ill. It was the work of women that allowed families to prosper economically.

Poor women also had to work outside of their homes. They were mostly small-scale merchants in public markets (agora). In Sparta, women had the right to indulge in athletic training just as men, but

Sparta was an exception. In the public life of a city, the women had important roles during funerals, religious holidays and rituals, and state festivities. Women who were priestesses enjoyed considerable prestige, which brought them certain benefits, such as a state salary and freedom of movement in public. Some of the religious cults were reserved for women, and they had their own all-women festivals and rites. By the 5th century, Athens alone had around forty such cults.

Upon marriage, a husband would take the role of a woman's legal guardian. This role was previously occupied by her father or another male relative if her father was absent. Marriages were officially arranged by men, but it was no secret that women would often take part in the negotiations. Girls as young as five years would be betrothed by their fathers. The engagement ceremony was an important public event, and it demanded the presence of several witnesses. However, the marriage itself would take place only when the woman reached a certain age, usually her early teens. The groom needed to be at least ten years old for a legal marriage. The marriage procession was similar to more modern marriage celebrations, with the bride going to live in her husband's house. The woman had to bring a dowry as well, which could be money or a part of her father's land. The dowry was her insurance, and the husband had to return it to her in case of a divorce. The divorce law ensured that a woman could leave her husband at her initiative, but the husband had every right to expel his wife from his household too.

Marriage equality ends here. Men were legally able to indulge in sexual intercourse outside of the marriage with prostitutes or slaves, both male or female, while women had no such freedoms. Adultery was punishable by law and applicable even to men caught in adultery with a married woman. Sparta was an exception here. Childless women were allowed to have multiple sexual partners to produce an heir as long as they had their husband's permission.

The guardianship over women came out of the Greeks' concern for procreation. The Greek men had a paternalistic attitude toward women because of their experience of the Greek Dark Ages when a sudden drop in the population led to an economic crash and poverty. A woman, as a child-bearer, had to endure the blame for what happened during the Dark Ages. She was often described as a necessary evil a man had to endure in order to procreate. This is even reflected in the Greek myth about Pandora, the first woman created by the gods. She was sent to mankind with a box filled with disease and evil. Her mischievous nature led her to open the box and unleash its contents on humanity. Many scholars today believe that the myth of Pandora was altered by later Greeks to justify the existence of a bad wife or to excuse their misogyny. Pandora went from a matriarchal goddess to a human woman and the bringer of evil and misfortune. Some even claim that this change marks the turn from a matriarchal Greek society to a patriarchal one. Nevertheless, to the ancient Greeks, Pandora and women were a necessary evil, as only through them can a man procreate. Having offspring was seen as a man's duty, and being childless was frowned upon.

Chapter 2: Oligarchy, Tyranny, and Democracy

Carved representation of Demos ("population") being crowned by Democracy (336 BCE) https://en.wikipedia.org/wiki/Athenian_democracy#/media/File:Demos_embodiment_being_crowned_by_Democracy._Ancient_Agora_Museum_in_Athens.jpg

The size and the influence of a state could have differed greatly. Among the most influential ones were Athens and Syracuse. Athens's territory was around 2,500 square kilometers (965 square miles), approximately the size of modern-day Luxembourg or California's

Orange County. The population of Athens varied greatly during the Classical period, but it can be estimated at around one-quarter of a million people. In comparison, the northern neighbor of Athens was Plataea, a state only 170 square kilometers (66 square miles) large, with a population below 10,000 people. And Plataea wasn't even the smallest Greek state. The smallest known one was on the island of Kea, which occupied only fifteen square kilometers (six square miles).

But no matter the size, the Greek poleis interacted with each other as if they were equal. Diplomatically, economically, and militarily, they were truly equal, but their power, wealth, and influence were different. Each of these state's political life developed independently, but over time, they came to share the most fundamental political institutions and social traditions. They shared the political disadvantage of women, slavery, the concept of citizenship, legal equality of those who held citizenship, and the social predominance of the wealthy elite.

Although the poleis shared political and social concepts, they developed them quite differently. The concept of a monarchy ended with the downfall of the Mycenaean civilization. The only place where a certain form of kingship survived was in Sparta, but even there, it was a unique system of dual kingship that was part of a more complex oligarchic system. In Sparta and some other city-states, meaningful political power was granted only to several individuals. This political system is known as an oligarchy (Greek *oligarkhia*—rule of the few). Other city-states were ruled by a tyrant, an individual who managed to grab all of the political power of a polis. Tyrants could pass their rule to their sons, but this was not a tradition. A tyrant could easily be replaced by another tyrant or a completely different political system.

Another early political system was a democracy, the rule of the people (Greek *demokratia*). Democracy meant giving all male citizens the power to participate in political life. The Greek democracy was an innovation of the late Archaic period that broke the rule of the previous people's assemblies. Even tyrants ruled with the existence of some kind of assembly or council that could influence political decisions. But democracy gave the people full freedom of political decision-making. Democracy came to dominate the political world of Greece during its Classical period, but it developed differently from polis to polis. Athenian democracy is renowned since it gave each citizen immense political power that extended into individual freedoms, something that was unprecedented in the ancient world.

The Political Development of Sparta

Sparta remains famous for its military society even today. But to maintain that defensive readiness, discipline, and military way of life, the Spartans had to come up with a political system that would support it and even strengthen it. Their answer was an oligarchy. Nestled between rugged mountains in the southeastern Peloponnese, the Spartans inhabited the region called Laconia (that is why they are sometimes referred to as Laconians or Lacedaemonians). Spartans had access to the sea, but their harbor, the Gytheion, opened into a very dangerous zone in the Mediterranean, so no one ever dared to sail there. Thus, Sparta was protected by its treacherous sea and the mountains, allowing it to develop perfect defenses.

The earliest Sparta was a commune of four villages that later developed into a polis. The political unification of the small settlements was called synoecism, which was how the polis of Sparta came to be. Synoecism allowed the people to continue living in their village even after unifying into a city-state. However, there were cases in which the people moved to live in one central location after the synoecism.

The unification of the villages that made Sparta allowed this polis to become the dominant one in Laconia. However, since two of the original villages dominated over the others, a dual kingship was formed. The kings were not only the military commanders of the city-state's army but also their supreme religious figures.

Even though they were called kings, they were not alone in governing Sparta. They weren't able to make any political decisions on their own because they weren't despots. Instead, leaders of the oligarchic political system governed the polis through various institutions. Sparta's political group was the "few," twenty-eight men who had to be over sixty years old. The two kings acted as their leaders. Together, the thirty men were called the council of elders (Gerousia), and they drafted Sparta's policies. But they could not do anything more than formulate proposals, as these would be submitted to a vote of an assembly consisting of all free adult males (the citizens). The citizens were expected to approve all the council's proposals, so rejections were rare. However, this was only because the council was able to withdraw the proposal if they concluded that the public did not like it.

The kings and the Gerousia were counterbalanced by a board of five individuals, who were elected annually. Their task was to oversee policy-making. Thus, they were called ephors, the overseers. Ephors had access to all the council and assembly meetings. They also had great judicial power, as it was their duty to exercise judgments and punishments. Not even kings were immune to the ephors' judicial powers. Because the main duty of the ephors was to secure the supremacy of the law, they diluted the oligarchic powers of the Gerousia and the kings. The ephors were obliged to swear an oath each month in the name of the polis and to the king, promising they would preserve his kingship if he obliged by his oath. Thus, the king had to swear an oath to the polis that he would follow the established laws of kingship.

The Spartans didn't write down their laws, but they were very much obedient to them. Tradition says that a leader, known as Lycurgus, reformed the Spartan laws, but there is no written evidence to confirm his existence or to even assign a date to his rule. All that modern history can say about Spartan laws is that they evolved during the period between 800 and 600 BCE. Spartan law was transferred from generation to generation due to Sparta's highly structured way of life and economy. This Spartan way of life was a necessity, as they lived surrounded by the peoples they conquered and enslaved and whom they exploited economically. The Spartans were generally outnumbered by their slaves and servants, so they had to constantly work on maintaining their superiority. This was why the Spartans turned into a society of soldiers, constantly ready for war. To achieve this military society, the Spartans reconstructed and transformed the traditional family and adopted a new set of values and laws to live by.

The enslaved people that the Spartans conquered continued to live in self-governed communities, but they were obliged to serve in the Spartan army and pay taxes to their superior neighbor. What separated them from the Spartans was the lack of citizen's rights. The conquered people were called the *perioikoi* (the neighbors), and it is possible, though never proven, that they never rebelled against Sparta because they were allowed to keep their freedom and their properties. But Sparta also had real slavery, and there was also a layer of society known as *helot* (the captured). It is unclear if the helots were slaves or a new social construction between slaves and free men. It is also unclear if they were an ethnic group or a social layer or maybe even both. Nevertheless, the helots were the most numerous in Laconia. The main concern of the Spartans was keeping them in check, and each fall, the Spartans would declare war on the helots to reduce their numbers. Helots did rebel, and they tried to improve their living conditions and rights, but with no success.

Helots worked the Spartan land and produced food. They also worked in households as servants, allowing the men of Sparta to devote themselves to training for possible warfare. Helots were also employed to carry heavy military equipment during wars. Sometimes they were even armed if the enemy's numbers surpassed those of Spartan soldiers, and they were promised freedom if they fought. But they lacked training, so they were often the first to die on the battlefield, never gaining their promised freedom. However, even those who survived were never allowed full citizenship, meaning they were stuck in political and social limbo.

The Spartan way of life meant keeping the army in tip-top shape. Boys were allowed to live at home with their parents until the age of seven. Then, they were sent to live with other males in communal spaces, similar to military barracks, where they would train, hunt, exercise, and learn Spartan values. They would remain in the communal barracks until the age of thirty. The sons of the royal family were exempted from this harsh training, probably to avoid the social crisis that would ensue if a member of a royal family would fail to survive childhood. And many Spartans did fail. Young boys were often injured or even killed by the harsh environment they had to endure. If they were disobedient, the punishments were so gruesome that many of them preferred death. The boys were also forced to abandon their sentiments for their family to become part of a larger society. This is why they had to call all older men "father" and to emphasize their loyalty to the community, not to their genetic family.

Women in Sparta had more freedom than any other Greek society. They were expected to keep themselves healthy in order to bear healthy children. This is why they were allowed to exercise together with the boys, even wearing minimal clothing while doing so. Women didn't labor in the households, as that was a job for the helots. However, women were the prime educators of young children, and they had to prepare their sons for the rough life that awaited them in the communal barracks. Women were also allowed to own land, and inheritance was always equally divided between brothers and sisters. In fact, women came to hold most of the Spartan land because the male population declined due to the constant wars.

Even though marriages were arranged at a young age, husbands and wives were not allowed to live together, mainly because males had to live in barracks until they were thirty. This is why women had more power and control over the households and why men were expected only to see their wives in short nightly visits to procreate. If a man was incapable of giving a child to his wife, she was free to have intercourse with other men. Producing children was very important because Sparta always had a pressing need for more men, which is why it was obligatory for men to marry.

The Rise of the Tyranny

The opposition to the oligarchy caused the tyrants to rise to power in the Greek states. Sparta was spared from experiencing tyranny during the ancient period. Tyranny first came to be in Corinth in 657 BCE. There, the Bacchiadae family ruled as oligarchs, and they brought prosperity to their polis, making it one of the most prosperous Archaic Greek cities. They were excellent shipbuilders, and other Greek states contracted their naval engineers. This allowed them to be among the first to establish colonies at Syracuse and Corcyra.

But the Bacchiadae were violent rulers, and although Corinth prospered, its citizens were not satisfied. One of the noble individuals, Cypselus, prepared to take over the government. He gained popularity with the population by displaying values such as courage, prudence, and philanthropy. He was the complete opposite of the violent Bacchiadae oligarchs. As he gained popular support, he easily persuaded the Oracle of Delphi to favor his ensuing rebellion. His popularity was such that once he took over power in Corinth, he was able to deal with his rivals easily and could walk the streets without bodyguards. Cypselus continued to reinforce Corinth's economy by starting pottery exports, mainly to Italy. He also founded many new colonies in the western poleis of the Mediterranean, which helped him to promote trade.

Cypselus died in around 625 BCE and was succeeded by Periander, his son. Although he continued his father's economic expansion of Corinth, Periander was a harsh ruler and didn't have the support of the people. Although he managed to stay in power until his death in 585, the hatred among his people was such that his successor, Psammetichus, was overthrown by the people. The tyranny in Corinth was short-lived, and it was swiftly replaced by eight magisters who had the help of a council, which consisted of eighty men.

But there is more to Greek tyranny than what Corinth experienced. What ancient Greeks called tyranny is not at all what a modern Western society would imagine. The ancient tyranny was a political system in which the head of one family would rule with the help of an elite layer of society, one that specialized in government, religion, and/or the military. Ancient tyranny is comparable to the modern-day concept of a monarchy but without hereditary succession (although it did happen). Although the rule was often passed from father to son, all tyrants were easily replaced by their rivals and enemies. When it comes to Greece during the mid-6th century BCE, though, tyrants would rarely be replaced with other tyrants. Instead, the people would rise against their ruler, and once they secured his downfall, they would not bring in another tyrant but would rather establish a citizen-centered government. Tyranny would rarely last for more than two generations, and it was never the same in the Greek cities.

Tyrants came to power by overthrowing their predecessors. But to do this, the Greek tyrants had to cultivate the support of the masses. These masses would make up a tyrant's army, and the ruler needed to keep them satisfied. As soon as he failed to do so, he was under threat of rebellion. To win over a great number of people, the tyrants would extend citizenship to those who were not eligible for it before. They also started public works to benefit the city-state and provide employment for their supporters. The tyrants worked in the interest of the people, and for that, they were rewarded with loyalty and support. But all tyrants had their rivals who wanted to overthrow them and take over the governance. Through the works and machinations of rivals, tyrants would often face a civil war. However, more often than not, the tyrants themselves would rule as oppressors, violently and brutally, which brought the wrath of their people upon themselves.

The Political Development of Athens

As Sparta came to be by synoecism of Laconian villages, so did Athens come to be by synoecism of Attica. Attica had several ports on its shores, and the Athenians were much better seafarers than the Spartans. This allowed them to communicate with other people and establish trade relations. Landlocked Sparta instead turned to conquest.

Tradition says Athens was founded by a hero named Theseus, who was an adventurer who defeated the Minotaur. The labors of Theseus became Athens's foundation myths, as the hero defeated many monsters and criminals to promote the moral institutions of his polis. Thus, Athenians were proud of their superior moral and civilized lives compared to the rest of the Greek world.

Just as the rest of Greece, Athens suffered a sudden population decline during the Greek Dark Ages. But archaeological evidence suggests that it had no trouble recovering from this destructive period of history. As early as 800 BCE, Athens's population started rising, and evidence found in various burial places proves the revival of agriculture.

From 800 to 700 BCE, the fastest-growing population of Attica was the free peasants. They worked the land and produced food, and they insisted on having a say in politics. Some of the peasants became wealthy landowners, gaining enough power to influence the elite families and demand political equality. At the time, these elite families ruled Athens in the form of a broad oligarchy. But the continuous rivalry among them prevented them from forming a united front against the pressure that came from the lower levels of society. The military strength of Athens completely depended on citizen militias, and the elite had to address the political pressure to ensure the survival of its army.

Already at this early stage of its political development, Athens was on the road toward democracy. By the late 7th century, all male citizens, rich or poor, had a share in governance, although not equal. Being this close to democracy, the Athenians had to prevent an individual from rising to the status of a tyrant. His name was Cylon, and in around 632 BCE, he attempted to overthrow the loose Athenian oligarchy and crown himself a tyrant. But the people wouldn't allow it. The population growth of Athens had given the power to the people, and they rallied against Cylon.

During the late 7th century, male freeborn Athenians had the right to attend state meetings. They were ruled by nine archons, who were elected each year. The archons were the oligarchs, and they had the power to render verdicts in disputes and criminal accusations, as well as to head the government. But every free male citizen had the right to be heard. Thus, the elite continued to rule Athens and secure their position as archons, but it was the assembly that elected the archons. The poor even had the right to join the assembly.

In 621, a man named Draco was elected as one of the archons, and he took it upon himself to establish Athens's code of laws (known as the Draconian laws), which would bring stability and equality to the polis. But he wasn't successful at all, as his laws only further destabilized Athens. Draco's laws were harsh, and they brought about the deterioration of the life of free peasants. This further undermined the social peace of Athens and brought forth an economic crisis in which the rich fought the peasants and the poor. Little is known of the Draconian laws except that the death sentence was introduced for all crimes. It is also known that they helped the rich accumulate even more riches and land, and the poor were forced to abandon farming and work for the rich so they could support their families. This led to lower production of food and an economic crash.

Soon, conditions became so bad that civil war threatened to engulf Athens. Desperate, Solon, the archon elected in 594, revised the Draconian laws and introduced a series of economic changes. He attempted to balance the political power between the rich and the poor by introducing four classes in which all male citizens were ranked. The classes were divided according to wealth into *pentakosiomedimnoi* (five-hundred-measure landowners), whose wealth brought much agricultural produce, *hippeis* (horsemen, or three-hundred-measure landowners), *zeugitai* (yoked-men, or two-hundred-measure landowners), and the *thetes* (the laborers, less than two-hundred-measure landowners). The higher the rank one had, the higher governmental offices he could occupy. The laborers were barred from all offices, although they were still eligible to participate in the assembly. Solon also gave the assembly legislative responsibilities, giving the laborers a foundation on which they would later build their political activities.

On an economic level, Solon canceled the income taxes, allowing the entrepreneurs to increase their wealth. Thus, social mobility was introduced, leading Athens one step closer to true democracy. If a man could increase his wealth through production or trade, he could climb the social ladder and increase his eligibility for a governmental office. Archaeologists found a statue erected to honor Anthemion, son of Diphilus. Anthemion was a man who climbed from the fourth to the second social rank. Originally a laborer, he became a horseman, gaining more political and social rights as time passed.

The poor were even more empowered by Solon, who gave every male citizen, regardless of his social rank, the power to accuse others and appeal cases. No longer was justice in the hands of the elite; rather, it belonged to all the people of Athens. Thus, Athens had one of the most developed political systems during the 6th century. All male citizens were able to participate meaningfully in the making of laws as well as in the administration of justice. Athens was so close to democracy, but fate would not allow it just yet.

From Tyranny to Democracy in Athens

Although Solon's reforms managed to elevate Athens above the ensuing civil war, the peace didn't last for long. A new conflict started because of the rivalries for offices and social status. The elites were fighting among themselves, and the poor continued to be dissatisfied. The outcome of the unrest that followed was Athens's tyranny. Pisistratus first rose as Athens's tyrant. He championed the interests of the poor while securing the support of his wealthy friends, ensuring his victory. But it took him three tries to establish himself as the ruler of Athens, doing so in 546 BCE. As soon as he started his rule, he modeled his tyranny on Corinth. He started promoting the economic, cultural, and architectural development of the polis, and he started exporting Athenian goods, mainly pottery.

Pisistratus was succeeded by his eldest son, Hippias, after his death in 527 BCE. Hippias introduced nepotism in Athens by making sure that his family members occupied the most important government roles. But to appease his rivals, he would sometimes allow them to serve as archons, keeping the jealousy among the elites in control, at least to a degree. The wealthy Alcmaeonid family proved to be a harder nut to crack. They were the tyrant's rivals, and they secured Sparta's help in their attempt to overthrow Hippias. The Alcmaeonids were able to do so because of a scandal that happened in Athens that resulted in the exile of many elite families.

In 514 BCE, Hipparchus, a younger brother of Hippias, was killed during the Panathenaic festival. The Greeks often portrayed this murder of the tyrant's brother as the "liberation act," a moment when Athens decided to overthrow its tyrant. But in reality, the murder was of a much more personal nature. It was committed by two Athenians, Harmodius and Aristogeiton, who were lovers. Harmodius had refused the amorous advances of Hipparchus. To retaliate, Hipparchus publicly insulted Harmodius's sister, and the young man felt obliged to defend his sister's honor. He killed the tyrant's brother but was immediately cut down by his bodyguards. It is unclear if

Aristogeiton had anything to do with the actual killing, but as Harmodius's lover, he was interrogated and killed. Hippias responded to his brother's murder by hardening his autocratic rule. He started ruling as a sole despot, relying on mercenaries to quell any resistance and exiling his political opponents.

The exiled Alcmaeonids heavily invested in the repair of Apollo's temple at Delphi. It was there that the Spartans first heard of Athens's troubles, for whenever they asked for divine guidance in their domestic affairs, the temple's answer would be "first free Athens." The Spartans didn't hesitate because acquiring Athens for their league would be a substantial addition. Besides, Hippias was at his most vulnerable. Nevertheless, it took Sparta two invasions of Attica and a siege of the Acropolis before Athens finally fell in 510 BCE. Hippias had to flee his city, and he sought refuge in Persia.

The Spartans were aware they wouldn't be able to directly control Athens as the city-state was equal in power to their own. Instead, the soldiers left the city immediately after overthrowing the tyrant, and the Spartans hoped the Athenian elite would see the benefits in harboring good relations. Unfortunately, the Athenian elite was deeply fragmented, and the Spartan king, Cleomenes I, put his man, Isagoras, as the head of Athens's pro-Sparta oligarchy. The leader of the aristocratic Alcmaeonid family, Cleisthenes, found himself representing the political opposition. He started his own coalition of elite families and even expanded it to include the common citizens of Athens. As Cleisthenes's coalition grew, Isagoras realized the threat it posed, and in 508 BCE, he called the Spartans. Cleisthenes was forced into exile, and according to Herodotus (a 5th-century Greek scholar), seven hundred families followed him. But when the Spartans came and Isagoras tried to disband the Athenian council, the Athenians took up arms. Isagoras and his Spartans suddenly found themselves on the defensive, and they were forced to retreat to the Acropolis. After a three-day-long siege, the Spartans surrendered and left Athens, with Isagoras in tow.

This Athenian revolt sparked major changes in state politics, and Cleisthenes managed to recognize the right moment to include ordinary citizens in politics. If it wasn't for his inclusion of the commoners in the coalition, Isagoras and the Spartans would have easily taken over the rule and gathered the Athenian elite into a dominant coalition. But the commoners changed the game. They found out that they were willing to bring about changes that would be in their favor. They were ready to take up arms and revolt.

After the expulsion of Isagoras and the Spartans, the Athenians were unwilling to go back to the old political system of the elite coalitions. Cleisthenes was recalled from his exile, and the people expected him to make good on his earlier promises of the expansion of citizens' rights. He also had to deal with the likelihood of Sparta's return to Attica. As emergency measures, Cleisthenes brought forth a series of reforms that were built on the civic identity of the Athenians. In essence, Cleisthenes invented democratic federalism, granting citizenship to all towns in the region of Attica. In the aftermath of the revolution, this political system proved to be a more successful political model than its inventor could have ever hoped. Thus, Cleisthenes started building a larger and stronger state in a territory that could have easily supported several independent poleis.

Furthermore, Cleisthenes issued a reformed constitution that expanded on the 139 villages and towns of Attica, by which the neighborhood of the region was divided into demes. This term is an Anglicized form of the original Greek *Demos*, which means the people. Therefore, the neighborhoods were divided based on how many people belonged to them. The Athenians were the *Demo*s (people) of Athens, and other neighborhoods had *Demos* of their own. Demes were different in size, but on average, they consisted of 15 to 250 male citizens, as only men could hold citizenship. Each citizen was treated on different levels: as a citizen of his deme and as a citizen of Athens. Acquiring citizenship was a complicated process because each male above eighteen years old had to be formally recognized by the assembly of his local deme as having been born by a father who held Athenian citizenship.

Apart from demes, Cleisthenes introduced a division of citizens by artificially created tribes. Each tribe consisted of roughly one-tenth of Attica's citizens, and the tribe's people were drawn from three different regions. That way, one deme would consist of only a third of one given tribe. That means that the tribes were regionally diverse, and these mixed-region tribes were the basis of Athens's civic affairs, such as the army, festivals, and public life.

The Council of 500 consisted of five hundred members, and they conducted Athens's day-to-day public affairs. The members were recruited from the described deme/tribe system. There is no evidence of the council's regulations in its early days, but later, each member was paid for his service, and he had to be at least thirty years old. Each year, the ten tribes would provide fifty counselors, chosen by a lot, amounting to five hundred altogether. The fifty chancellors were chosen from different demes, with each deme sending a different number depending on the size of its population.

The councilors were not the representatives of their demes or their tribe's interests. They were expected to serve all citizens of Attica equally and represent the collective knowledge of Athens's population. The councilors' service was limited to only two non-consecutive years, making it a common experience for all Athenian men. Socrates, a philosopher who often emphasized his uninterest in public life, served as the councilor of Alopece, although only at the advanced age of sixty-three.

Athens's also had a second council, the Areopagus, named after the hill where the council would meet. Its members were chosen among the ex-magistrates, and they played a significant role in domestic politics after the revolution. However, the Areopagus survived only one generation after Cleisthenes's reforms, as the Council of 500 became dominant and, in time, the only Athenian body of government. But the legislative power continued to lay with the citizen assembly, which, together with the Council of 500, represented the earliest forms of Athens's democracy.

Chapter 3: The Persian Wars (499–449 BCE)

Persian king killing a Greek soldier, relief dated to 475 BCE
https://en.wikipedia.org/wiki/Battle_of_Thermopylae#/media/File: Achaemenid_king_killing_a_Greek_hoplite.jpg

The Athenians were worried that the Spartans would come back to defend the oligarchy they had installed. In 507 BCE, they asked King Darius I of Persia for help in the form of a protective alliance. At this point in history, the Persian Empire was the largest, most powerful, and richest state in the ancient world. Herodotus claims that when the Athenian delegates asked for the alliance, the Persian representatives mockingly asked them who they were and where they came from, symbolizing Athens's insignificance in Persia. Nevertheless, in just two generations, Athens would come to control vast lands, known today as the Athenian empire. This transformation from an insignificant power to one of the world's leading powers was swift, and it marks the beginning of the Classical period, an age in Greek history that modern scholars believe started around 500 BCE and ended after the death of Alexander the Great in 323 BCE.

Previously, Persia extended its borders westward and took over the whole of Anatolia and many Greek poleis on its shores. The people of mainland Greece had every right to fear the expanding Persian Empire, as its intention was unclear. The Persians didn't know much about the Greeks, and the Greeks knew very little about the Persians. This mutual ignorance proved to be the reason behind many explosive misunderstandings that would lead to some of the most famous conflicts in world history.

The Athenian delegation to Sardis, where they met the Persian representatives, knew that they needed to recognize Darius I's superiority. But what they couldn't understand, or probably didn't know, was that Persia would never accept a Greek model of alliance where both sides were equal partners. Darius I expected Athens to bow to him. The Athenian delegation, having no other options, accepted the humiliating terms of the alliance, but the Athenian assembly was outraged. They refused the alliance but failed to send another delegation to Persia to inform them of the breaking of the pact. This diplomatic failure led Athens to continue believing in its independence, while Persia already counted on its loyalty and deference. This misunderstanding started a series of misfortunate events that would end in the Persian invasion of mainland Greece. The wars that ensued forced some of the mainland Greek city-states to work together, even though they saw each other as hostile or even enemies.

The heartland of the Persian Empire was in today's southeast Iran. By the time of Darius I (550-486 BCE), it covered a vast territory from modern-day Afghanistan to Turkey and north-south from the border of Russia to Egypt and the Indian Ocean. Its population was heterogeneous, and it counted millions. The administration of such a vast empire was based on satraps, who ruled smaller territories without the direct influence of the king. The satraps' duties were to raise an army when needed, keep order in their lands, and send annual taxes and revenues to the royal treasury. The taxes were paid in money, food, raw materials, valuable commodities, etc., and all of it greatly increased the wealth and prestige of the Persian rulers. Thus, the Persian monarch was probably the richest individual in the known world. Even the Greeks were awed by the wealth and lavishness of the Persian court, and they referred to the Persian monarchs as the "Great Kings."

The Outbreak of the War

The Persian Wars were a series of conflicts between Persia and Greece during the early Classical period. They took place during the 490s, as well as from 480 to 479 BCE.

The conflicts first started with the revolt of the Ionian (a region in western Anatolia, not to be confused with the Ionian Sea) Greek city-states against the Persian rule. The Ionian Greeks had lost their freedom to the Kingdom of Lydia, which overpowered them during the reign of its King Croesus (560-546 BCE). The Lydians then wanted to claim the rest of Anatolia, which was already under Persian rule. Croesus attacked Persia in 546 BCE, but he was defeated, and he lost all of his territories, including Ionia, to King Cyrus of Persia. The Persians installed tyrants in Ionia, who provoked the Greeks to revolt. The Ionians sent a delegation to mainland Greece asking for help in their effort to overthrow Persian rule. Sparta refused to help because its king, Cleomenes, saw no reason to fight against an empire whose capital was so far away that it would take his army at least three months to reach it. But unlike Sparta, Athens agreed to help, sending military aid first to neighboring Eretria on the island of Euboea and then to Ionia. The Athenian army reached Sardis and burned it to the ground. They roused the Persians' wrath, and they hurried home, but the Persian counterattack in Ionia made the Greek allies lose their coordination. By 494 BCE, the Ionian revolt had been completely crushed.

To prevent Ionia from rising against his rule again, Darius I sent his officer, Mardonius, to reorganize its administration. The result was the admission of democracy in some of the Ionian Greek city-states where tyrannies had previously been in place. But when Darius I learned about Athens's involvement in the burning of Sardis, he was outraged and wanted revenge. The Greeks were insignificant in his opinion, and he had no grand scheme of conquering the Greek mainland, but he desired to punish those who dared attack his territory. If it is to be believed, the historian Herodotus says that Darius ordered one of his slaves to say to him "Remember the Athenians" three times before a meal every day.

To punish the Greeks, Darius sent a flotilla of ships in 490 BCE. Eretria was burned before the Persian troops disembarked on the northeastern coast of Attica. Among the Persians was Hippias, who was now old but still hopeful he would be reinstalled as an Athenian tyrant. The Athenian army was greatly outnumbered, and the men were forced to ask Sparta and other Greek city-states for help. The courier who was dispatched to Sparta became famous, as he ran 140 miles (225 kilometers) from Athens to Sparta in less than two days. He then ran back to Marathon, where a battle between Athens and Persia was taking place, and then ran back to Athens to declare the Athenian victory. After doing so, he collapsed from exhaustion and died. It is incredibly likely that none of this happened or that events have been blended together. Regardless, the runner was the inspiration for the marathon in the modern-day Olympic Games, which is twenty-five miles (forty kilometers) long, the approximate distance from Marathon to Athens.

In the Battle of Marathon, Athens had the help of a small contingent sent by neighboring Plataea. Against all odds, the Greek army managed to defeat the Persians and marched quickly back to Athens to stop the Persian fleet from attacking their city from the sea. The march was another impossible task, but the Athenians managed to complete it, despite being exhausted by the battle and carrying heavy gear. Their march, in combination with the runner to Sparta, is today celebrated as a marathon race, with major cities around the world organizing similar events every year.

The Persians were forced to return home without taking Athens. But the Greek victory barely affected Persia's might. Back home, Darius had more than enough manpower and resources to crush the whole of Greece. Nevertheless, the Athenians celebrated their victory, as they had proved they were able to fight and defeat a much superior enemy. The symbolism of the victory at Marathon outweighed its military significance. Darius I was outraged, not because the Greeks threatened his empire but because his prestige was suffering. The ordinary men of Athens had managed to take up arms and defend their freedom. The unexpected victory boosted the self-esteem of the Athenians, and they celebrated their victory at Marathon for decades to come.

The Persian Invasion

With their newly gained confidence, the Athenians decided to join the resistance against the Persian invasion of Greece that came in 480 BCE. Darius vowed he would conquer Greece as revenge for the insult to his prestige. However, it took so much time to gather the Persian forces from all the corners of the vast empire that by the time the army was ready, Darius had died. However, the invasion plans weren't abandoned. His son, Xerxes I (518–465 BCE), led the invasion of the Greek mainland. His army was huge, and it consisted of infantry and ships. In fact, Xerxes expected that the Greeks would surrender once they saw the might of his armies. The city-states of northern and central Greece did just that. They were in the direct line of the Persian advance, and they were aware they stood no chance in an open fight. Some of the cities, such as Thebes (in Boeotia, not to be confused with Thebes in Egypt), openly supported the Persian invasion, hoping to gain political and economic advantages once the fighting was over and Xerxes had secured his victory.

The remaining thirty-one Greek poleis, mostly in the southern regions, organized an alliance to defend themselves from Persian attacks. Because Sparta was a military state, it was chosen as the leader of the new military coalition. Syracuse was supposed to join the coalition, but its tyrant, Gelon, demanded the command of all the Greek forces, but both the Spartans and Athenians had refused him.

The first encounter between the coalition and the Persian army became one of the most famous battles in the history of the world. It occurred at Thermopylae, a narrow mountain pass on the eastern coast of central Greece. There, seven thousand Greek soldiers met a Persian army that numbered, according to Herodotus, a million. Modern scholars believe that the numbers were greatly exaggerated by contemporary historians and that it is more likely there were around 150,000 Persians. Nevertheless, the Greeks were once again greatly outnumbered, but they managed to hold the pass and block the Persian invasion for seven days. In the end, they were betrayed by one Greek soldier, Ephialtes, who hoped the Persians would reward him for showing them a secret path that would bring their army behind the Greek ranks. Upon hearing about the betrayal, King Leonidas I of Sparta took three hundred of his soldiers and guarded the Greek army's flank, allowing it to retreat to safety and fight another day. The legend of the 300 has its origin in this episode of the Battle of Thermopylae, but the truth is that the Spartans were joined by 700 Thespians, 900 helots, and 400 Thebans in this defense. Still, they were outnumbered, and they fought until all of them were killed, after which the Persians took over Thermopylae.

The Battle of Thermopylae is famous, but it's not the only battle that was fought at that time. It was a part of a two-front conflict, and it played out together with the naval battle at Artemisium. The alliance of Greek poleis gathered their fleets, although they had a much smaller number of ships than the Persians. The Persian naval force had started at 1,200 ships, but one-third of them were lost at sea early on. Another two hundred shipwrecked when they departed to sail around the Greek fleet and trap it. The naval battle lasted for three days, and both sides lost an equal number of ships. However, the Greek alliance couldn't afford such losses because they had a smaller fleet to begin with. The overall tactics to fend off the Persian invasion involved holding both positions at Thermopylae and the sea. Once the news of the defeat at Thermopylae reached the allied navy, the Greeks decided to retreat to Salamis, located in the Saronic Gulf (sixteen kilometers, or ten miles, away from Athens). The Persians finally had an open passage to Attica, and they quickly captured Athens. But the city had already been evacuated, with women, children, and non-combatants retreating to the northeastern coast of the Peloponnese.

The Persians pursued the Greeks, and another battle occurred in 481 BCE: the Battle of Salamis. Just as at Thermopylae, the Greek allies decided to use their country's geography to defend themselves. The channel at Salamis was too narrow for the Persians to use all of their ships at once, and it greatly restricted their maneuverability. The heavy Greek ships were able to use their underwater rams to sink the smaller Persian ones. Of all of Xerxes's army, only Artemisia I of Caria, Queen of Halicarnassus and general of her fleet of five ships, was against a Persian attack on Salamis. She was wise enough to see the trap the Greeks were preparing, but Xerxes listened to his other advisors, who urged him to attack the Greeks while the victory of Artemisium was still fresh. Artemisia was a great commander, and she fought well during the Battle of Salamis, so much so that Xerxes praised her, saying how his men became women and women became men. In truth, Artemisia was clever, and it seems she fought only for the survival of her ships. She was famous for carrying two flags, and she would pursue Greek ships under the Persian flag. But if she was pursued by the enemy, she would display a Greek flag so the pursuer would abandon his chase. These tactics allowed her to survive, and after the Battle of Salamis, Xerxes recognized her as his best naval officer and awarded her with Greek armor. According to Herodotus, it was Artemisia who advised Xerxes to retreat to Asia Minor and leave his general, Mardonius, with the Persian army to fight the Greeks another day. Xerxes listened to her advice. Following the Greek victory at Salamis, he retreated.

Mardonius remained with 300,000 Persian soldiers, and he told the Athenians that if they capitulated, they could become Persian satraps and rule over the other Greeks. The Athenians refused, and their city was sacked once more. The next year, in 479 BCE, the Greek army, led by a Spartan commander and prince named Pausanias (520-470 BCE), fought the Persians at the Battle of Plataea in Boeotia. At the same time, the Greek fleet fought at Mycale in Ionia. The Greek alliance was successful on both fronts this time and managed to defend its homeland against the invading Persians. They fought the richest and most powerful empire in the world and were able to defeat it. The Greeks had superior weapons and armor, and their use of the topography helped them achieve these victories against an enemy that easily outnumbered them. Thirty-one Greek city-states fought as if they belonged to the same political entity. The rich, the poor, and even some of the women showed remarkable courage when facing the mighty enemy of Persia. Their willingness to fight and preserve their independence came from the new ideals of political freedom that sprouted at the end of the Archaic period.

Chapter 4: The Rise of Athens and the Delian League

The Parthenon as seen today
*https://en.wikipedia.org/wiki/Acropolis_of_Athens#/media/File:
The_Parthenon_in_Athens.jpg*

The Greek alliance managed to preserve the freedom of mainland Greece, but it also achieved something unimaginable. Athens and Sparta left their old rivalries behind and joined the alliance together with the other Greek city-states. Athens and Sparta also managed to share the leadership of the alliance without any internal conflicts. Athens provided most of the fleet and funds, as Attica had a huge source of silver at the time, while Sparta gave its infantry, as well as many capable generals and officers.

But once the Persians were gone, the Greek leaders found themselves unable to maintain their cooperation. There were many Athenians who believed that the two poleis should work together for the mutual good. They started pro-Sparta lobbying during the Athenian assembly, but it wasn't enough. Instead, Athens came to rule the alliance of the city-states that took part in the defense against the Persians. This was the start of the Athenian empire, one of the most fascinating of paradoxes. The Greek city-states defended their ideals of freedom when they were fighting the Persians only to allow Athens to rise to power. Other city-states willingly subjected themselves to Athens and gave it the means to start oppressing them.

But to understand how this happened, one must understand the circumstances in mainland Greece that ensued right after the Persian Wars. The Greeks were afraid the Persians would be back and attempt another conquest of their homeland. They were also afraid that another conflict such as the Persian Wars would lead to the economic downfall of the whole of Greece. The Greeks of the Aegean Islands had even more reason to fear. They were in close proximity to the Persian Empire, and if Xerxes decided to retaliate for the loss, they would be the first to receive the blow.

The conflict continued in 478, but this time, the Greek alliance set sail to liberate the coastal cities of Ionia, as well as in Cyprus. They even laid siege to Byzantium, a Greek colony at the time. But these efforts weren't as productive as the defense of the Greek mainland, mostly because the Spartan commander Pausanias behaved offensively toward the Ionians in the alliance. He was quickly recalled back to Sparta to answer the charges against him. The Ionians asked the Athenians to take over the command, and a new military alliance started, known as the Delian League. The name is a modern invention; modern scholars believed the treasury of the league was on the island of Delos, hence the name.

The Spartans thought of the Athenians as friendly allies, and they were more than glad to let Athens take over the leadership, mostly because they wanted to retreat from the conflict with Persia but also because they were afraid that any Spartan commander they would send would end up being as corrupt as Pausanias. Spartan leaders often displayed behavioral issues when in command of the armies of other poleis. This was probably due to the oppression they experienced during their training days in boyhood. Spartan life and the sense of authority were not mirrored in other city-state's armies, and Sparta was well aware of that. Anyway, Sparta had an ongoing need to keep its army at home and keep the helot revolts under control.

The member states of the Delian League took an oath never to leave the coalition. The islands of the Aegean Sea were the majority in the league, but the members also included the poleis of central Greece, as well as western Anatolia. The city-states of the Peloponnese remained in an alliance with Sparta. They were in an alliance long before the Persian Wars, and they wanted to maintain their loyalty. Athens and Sparta once again found themselves opposing each other, and each was a leader of a different military alliance. The Spartan alliance was named the Peloponnesian League by modern historians, and they shared an assembly that was tasked with setting the league's policies. But no action could be taken without the approval of the Spartan kings. The Delian League also had an assembly, and the idea was to reach decisions together. But in practice, Athens had the final word.

Athens wasn't offered the leadership of the Delian League because it was thought to have advanced leadership skills compared to other city-states but rather because it could provide the most resources, men, and ships. The Delian League's economy was structured in such a way that bigger poleis would provide whole ships with crews and more resources and money than the smaller city-states. The smaller poleis were allowed to group their resources to be able to provide ships and crews.

The Delian League was a naval alliance, so they needed warships. At the time, Greek warships were narrow vessels built for speed. Crews numbered up to 200 men, out of which 170 were rowers. The rest were officers, hoplite warriors, and archers who would engage the enemy's crew if needed. Over time, most of the member cities of the Delian League preferred to pay their dues in money instead of building ships. They had no capacity to build and equip warships, and it was easier to pay money. Only Athens, which was far larger than any of the other members of the Delian League, had engineers, crews, and shipyards, and it had the capacity of supplying the alliance with warships. The poorest of the Athenians served as rowers, but this servitude brought them money, as well as increased political influence, allowing them to elevate socially.

It was because of the superiority of Athens and its huge contribution to the Delian League that the smaller members lost their influence in decision-making. Even if they disagreed with Athens's proposals, they had no option but to accept them. If they proved to be stubborn, Athens would simply dispatch its fleet and attack them to persuade them to remain within the league and pay their dues. The Athenian men found themselves wielding enormous power, and soon enough, the dues became compulsory, more relatable to a tribute from vassal states than a membership fee. But once Athens subdued the rebellious members of the league, it became unpopular, as it would take away the political freedoms of other city-states. In 465 BCE, Thasos, an island in the northern Aegean Sea, withdrew from the Delian League. They did so because of the ongoing dispute with Athens over the control of gold mines in the mainland. To make them stay within the league, Athens led the alliance into a long siege of Thasos, ending it only in 463 BCE. The island was compelled to surrender to avoid the starvation of its populace. The punishment was harsh, as Athens made Thasos give up its whole fleet and pay enormous tribute to the league.

But the main goals of the Delian League were to expel the Persians from the city-states along the northeastern coast of the Aegean Sea. In just twenty years after the Battle of Salamis, the Delian League achieved this, and it even expelled the Persian fleet from the Aegean, ending its threat to Greece, at least for the next fifty years. Athens grew stronger and richer due to the many spoils that came from Persian defeats. By the middle of the 5th century BCE, all the members of the league together paid an equivalent of $200 million (in contemporary terms) annually. Athens had only around thirty thousand to forty thousand adult male citizens at the time, and this amount of income meant the general prosperity of the Athenian population. The expenditure was decided by the male citizens who attended the assembly, and most of the money was spent on maintaining the fleet. Both rich and poor citizens understood the value of the fleet, as it made them the mightiest polis. But the income was also spent on repairing the city's walls, roads, and public buildings.

Democracy in the Empire

The empire and democracy coexisted. Remember, the Athenian empire wasn't an actual empire. It was named that by modern scholars to mark the period of Athens's predominance in Greece. Athens did rule over the other members of the Delian League but never officially. This is why democracy was allowed to develop in certain parts of Greece, even though they were under Athens's control. Greek democracy had a gradual development, and it was based on a very simple principle: those who were able to provide an army should have political rights and power. But in Athens, the men who were in the army were not the elites. They were hoplites who fought on land and the *thetes* who rowed the boats during the naval battles. After the Persian Wars, these men were granted political power, and they were the majority of the adult citizens. They were called the *demos*, the commoners, and they gained sovereignty for the assembly. The political offices that had once held great power and prestige were now diminished in importance.

Due to the proposal of one individual, Pericles (495-429 BCE), the offices that were now open to the *demos* received a daily stipend financed by the state. This was the first time in the history of Greece that government representatives received state-funded salaries. This was because the majority of the *demos* were poor, and they were unable to leave their regular jobs to attend government meetings. They had to take care of their livelihoods and their families. In contrast, the board of military generals (ten members), who were also the most influential public officials, were elected annually and received no state-funded stipend. The stipend that the *demos* received for their participation in government was not lavish. It was equal to what a laborer could earn in one day. Nevertheless, it allowed the commoners to assume the political power that belonged to them. Pericles himself was a member of the elite, and he had no personal gain with the reform he introduced. But like Cleisthenes before him (who was Pericles's ancestor), Pericles worked to strengthen the egalitarian tendencies of Athenian democracy.

Pericles became extremely popular due to his introduction of the stipend for the *demos*. This is why he was able to push for other reforms, both in foreign and domestic policies, starting around 450 BCE. In 451 BCE, he introduced a new law of citizenship, making it available only to the individuals whose mother and father were born Athenians. Previously, citizenship was granted to those of Athenian fathers and non-Athenian mothers. Pericles did this to emphasize the importance and prestige of Athenian citizenship but also to elevate the status of Athenian women. Suddenly, the citizenship of women became important, and although they still had no political power, it brought a new level of prestige to females. After the introduction of the new law, a review of all-male citizenship had to be done to expel those who claimed it without grounds. This significantly reduced the number of people eligible to involve themselves in Athenian politics.

In foreign policy, Pericles's influence is less clear. During the 450s, Athens offered support to Egypt's rebellion, in which they tried to get rid of Persian rule. Athens raised a large army that was sent to Egypt, but the expedition proved to be an utter failure. More than two hundred ships were lost, together with their crews. Some of the lost rowers and soldiers were not Athenian but members of the Delian League. Nevertheless, the loss of manpower prompted Athens to be more careful, and it moved the league's treasury from Delos to Athens. This way, if the Persians decided to retaliate, the treasury would be safe. And it also gave Athens direct control over the Delian League's funds.

While Pericles's influences on foreign politics involving Persia are not known, he did support foreign policy against Spartan interests in Greece. In 457 BCE, at the Battle of Tanagra in Boeotia, the Athenian forces were defeated by the Peloponnesian League. However, in the following years, Athens took control of the region, as well as of neighboring Phocis. Victories were also achieved against Corinth and some of the island poleis of the Aegean Sea. But there was no enduring victory over Sparta and its allies, and by 447, Athens had lost control over Boeotia and Phocis. The next winter, Pericles agreed to a peace with Sparta, and a treaty was signed that froze the conflict between the two city-states for the next thirty years. Pericles had to do this because his political rivals in Athens started gaining momentum, and he needed to concentrate on dealing with them.

In 443, Pericles secured his political power in Athens by removing his main rival, a man named Thucydides. Pericles was elected as the general for the fifteenth year in a row, and no one could dispute his political influence. He was directly responsible for a war against one of the member states of the Delian League in 441 BCE when he rashly took a side in the political crisis of Samos. The conflict lasted until 439 BCE, and its main cause was that Samos wanted to leave the league as there was no longer a need to defend Greece from Persia. Athens wanted to retain its dominion over the allies, claiming that Persia was dormant only because of the league's existence. Samos wasn't the only city-state that rebelled against Athens at the time. Many poleis wanted to break off from the alliance, but Athens wouldn't let them. After all, Athens came to depend on the money the member states were sending as their part to the league.

Athens's Prosperity

Athens reached its golden age in the decades before the Peloponnesian War (431-404 BCE). During these years, Athens was at the height of its power and prosperity, and its communal abundance was shared by all of its citizens. However, the Athenians remained relatively modest, which can be seen in the unchanged house and farmhouse sizes. The villages were still tightly inhabited, and the urban center of Athens continued to have houses wedged against each other, occupying small spaces. The elite residences followed a similar design, with grouped bedrooms, dining rooms, a kitchen, and workrooms all gathered around an open courtyard in the center of the household. At this period, paintings and art were not yet displayed in the houses, not even in the residences of the richest Athenians. Furnishings were sparse and simple, without much difference between different social classes.

The rich were the benefactors of the public works, and Athens started landscaping its urban environment. The heart of the city had planted trees that would provide shade. Stoas were built at the edges of markets and the urban center. The stoas were decorated shelters that protected people from storms, rain, or the sun. The most famous one is the Painted Stoa, located at the central public square known as the Agora. There, people would gather to discuss local affairs and politics. The paintings on the walls of this stoa displayed some of the most famous scenes in Greek history, such as the Battle of Marathon.

Athens's wealth wasn't only due to the accumulation of the dues from the member states of the Delian League. The city received substantial revenues from harbor fees and sales taxes as well. Nevertheless, Athenians kept to their small-scale buildings, as they saw no need for lavish and monumental public works. The assembly gathered under the open sky, and they needed no building. Only a small raised speaker's platform was installed for the assembly. The first great project of the Classical period started in 447 BCE at Pericles's initiative—the buildings of Athens's Acropolis. There, he built two temples dedicated to Athena: the Parthenon and the Temple of Athena Nike. He also built a monumental gateway to the Acropolis known as the Propylaea and yet another temple dedicated to both Athena and Poseidon, known as the Erechtheion. But Pericles didn't use his own money to fund this project; rather, he used public funds. The cost of these enormous buildings was massive, and many of his political enemies scolded him for spending so much of the public funds.

The Athenians saw the building of the Acropolis as a symbol of their victory over the Persians, who had destroyed the previous temple to Athena that stood there. The old temple had an olive tree in its center, which symbolized Athena as the protector of agriculture, thus Athens. But after the Persian Wars, Athena gained new symbolism. She transformed into a warrior goddess of victory (Nike in ancient Greek). That is why the Parthenon used to house a large gold and ivory statue of Athena in body armor holding a statue of Nike. The Greek temples were not gathering places for worshipers but rather the houses for the divine. That is why Parthenon's design represents the standard Greek architecture of the period—a box with columns and various entrances. The columns were of Doric style, with simple carvings, not as elaborate as the Ionic style, which is often imitated in modern architecture. The temple was open only to priests and priestesses, but on occasion, it would open its doors for public religious ceremonies. The Parthenon alone was constructed of twenty thousand tons of Attica's marble, and it had sixty-five columns in total supporting it. True to the classical Greek style, the Parthenon has no straight lines or right angles.

Athens was the only city-state of classical Greece to build such a lavish temple. Greeks, in general, preferred to keep their public buildings designed for their purposes, not for their looks. But Athens wanted to emphasize its relationship with its patron goddess, and this can also be observed on the carvings that run along the walls of the Parthenon right under its roof. Here, the citizens of Athens were depicted in the company of the gods, even though it was clear there was no interaction between them. After all, the citizens of Athens were only humans, and the mighty gods were invisible and mysterious. But the sheer presence of citizens in the carvings of the Parthenon represents the special relationship the city had with the Greek gods, who always favored Athens. This is why the Athenians believed they were able to repel the Persians in the first place because the gods loved them above all else. Their success against the Persians was proof enough that the gods were on their side.

Chapter 5: Culture and Society of Classical Athens

An ancient Greek relief depicting all twelve Olympian gods
https://en.wikipedia.org/wiki/Twelve_Olympians#/media/File:Greek_-_Procession_of_Twelve_Gods_and_Goddesses_-_Walters_2340.jpg

The whole history of classical Greece in the 5th century BCE revolves around Athens. The city wasn't only the dominant political entity of Greece but also the most prestigious and developed, both culturally and socially. The mid-5th century was the Athenian golden age, and not a single other city-state has a similar amount of archaeological or written sources. This is why modern history mainly focuses on Athens when it comes to the discussion of classical Greece. But the archaeological findings of Athens and the focus put on this city by various scholars mustn't be taken as a substitution for the whole of

Greece. Athens doesn't equal Greece when talking about this period. Athens was a part of the Greek world, albeit the most developed and prominent one.

The Athenian dominance of the Greek world was no accident. It came as a result of many social and cultural changes of the mid-5th century. But while going through these changes, Athenian life remained unchanged. What came out of it was a sense of continuity in social matters, but there were also cultural innovations and ensuing tensions, which proved to be both destructive and creative. Publicly-supported arts gave birth to the tragic drama, which explored many serious, ethical issues of the period. The new form of education in classical Greece came into existence, but it found opposition among the traditionalists. For rich women, public life remained closed or at least limited by the old traditions of modesty and exclusion from political life. However, poor women gained access to public life simply because they had to work to support their families. The interplay of new and traditional was tolerated until the conflict with Sparta was renewed. This conflict pushed Athens into the Peloponnesian War, allowing the Athenian society to reach its breaking point. But behind everything that was happening in the cultural and social life of Athens lay religion.

Religion in Classical Greece

The main postulate of ancient Greek religion was that the humans, as a group but also as individuals, praised the gods and thanked them for the blessings they received. As seen in the previous chapter, the Athenians thought they had a special relationship with the gods, and they believed they were their favorites. Because of this, they were willing to spend huge amounts of money and goods to honor the gods through monuments or public religious ceremonies. The ceremonies often included sacrifices, gifts to the sanctuaries and temples, prayers, dances, songs, and processions. The individuals gifted the temples and sanctuaries, expecting the gods to repay them—a service for a service. The Greek understanding of the divine is underlain by the idea of mutual benefit between gods and humans. The gods didn't love humans as modern religions often teach. They only rewarded those who respected and honored them. The humans who offended the gods were punished as individuals (disease, death, suffering, etc.) or as a community (quakes, famine, loss in a war, etc.).

The gods' expectations were codified as rules of proper behavior for humans. Thus, humans didn't have to question what would offend the gods and what would please them. For example, the most cherished value that humanity possessed was hospitality toward guests. This value pleased the gods, but arrogance and violence displeased them. The Greeks believed that through dreams, oracles, and divinations, the gods communicated their displeasure to humans. The most common offenses were forgetting an offering for the gods or violating a sanctuary in enemy territory. It was believed that the gods didn't care much about common crimes and would leave humans to police themselves. But breaking an oath made toward fellow humans was a very serious religious offense, and it angered the gods. Homicide was considered the only common crime that offended the gods, and the gods would pollute the whole society to punish the murderer. Society could cleanse itself only by punishing the murderer.

The Greek gods were seen as carefree and immortal. They had easy lives, although they did know pain, usually produced from the dealings they had with the other gods or with humans. The Greek pantheon had the twelve most important gods, with Zeus as their leader. They would gather on the top of Mount Olympus to enjoy lavish banquets. The main thing that concerned the gods was their honor, and just like humans, the gods had to go to lengths to preserve it.

In order to communicate with the gods, the people had to sing hymns, praise them, offer sacrifices, or pray to them. Individuals worshiped gods and laid offerings for them at their homes in the company of the whole family and even the household. Temples were reserved for group ceremonies, which were headed by priests and priestesses. The clergy was chosen from the main citizen's body, meaning they led civil lives too. However, they rarely sought to engage in the political and social matters of the city-state. The special knowledge they possessed involved the performance of the ceremonies according to tradition, but they were never seen as guardians of a doctrine (as modern Christian priests and monks are often seen) because there wasn't any.

Not all the people joined every ceremony, nor were they obliged to. There were ceremonies specific to men and women, joint ceremonies, or those reserved only to married women or virgins. Laborers had a specific number of free days that they could use to attend religious ceremonies and offer sacrifices. Sacrifice was seen as one of the highest honors to the gods, but it wasn't a human sacrifice. The Greeks offered anything from grain, milk, and cakes to slaughtered animals. The sacrificed animals were symbolically given to the gods, and the humans would enjoy the meat on special occasions. Cattle were rare in ancient Greece; therefore, animal sacrifices usually occurred only during a time of great need or during large public ceremonies.

Ancient Greeks also enjoyed religious activities outside of the cults. They celebrated births and weddings and mourned the dead. Both rich and poor started giving offerings to their ancestors during the Classical period. Before this, rituals were mainly practiced by the rich. Everyone was allowed to consult the seers to decipher the meaning behind dreams or to ask for a magical spell that would help them with their love life or lift a curse. Hero cults were also widespread because the Greeks believed that the remains of prominent persons, usually from the distant past, retained special powers. But unlike the gods' powers, a hero's power was local, influencing only the polis in which he was buried. This is why bringing back the remains of heroes who died far away from their polis was important. In 475 BCE, Cimon (an Athenian general and statesman) brought what was believed to be the remains of Theseus to Athens. He was the founder of Athens and the hero who fought the Minotaur. The arrival of his remains to Athens was celebrated as a major event, and a new special shrine was erected for him in the city's center.

The most revered international cult was that of Demeter and Persephone, Demeter's daughter. The rite of the cult, in which its members had to take part, was the Mysteries, and everyone had the right to be initiated in the cult, no matter his or her origin. Even some slaves were granted the right of initiation through their service to Demeter's temple. The importance of the Eleusinian Mysteries was so great that an agreement between poleis was set to withhold from any conflict during a period of five days before the ceremonies. This way, everyone was guaranteed safe passage to join the festivities and ceremonies, which were held in Eleusis (hence Eleusinian Mysteries) in west Attica. The central event of the Mysteries was the revelation of Demeter's secret. Although the rite itself was described in detail, and we know what it involved, no one ever revealed what Demeter's secret was. The knowledge of it remains lost, and the only thing we can say with certainty is that it involved something the cult members had to do, say, and see. But this secrecy only serves as proof of how serious the cult of Demeter was taken and how dedicated the Greeks were to it.

The Eleusinian Mysteries were not the only initiation rites, nor was the cult of Demeter the most prominent one. There were many others, but this one perfectly depicts the ancient Greeks' devotion to their religion and rites. The Demeter and Persephone cult was an agrarian cult that symbolized the death and rebirth of nature. Other cults placed emphasis on the protection of people from disease, war, ghosts, poverty, or anything that could bring about individual or group suffering. The Greek gods were good and evil at the same time, just as humans were (and still are). In many ways, they were mirroring human behavior, so they shared human nature. This is why ancient Greeks didn't have a concept of a paradise or utopia that would rise on earth once the evil forces were banished. The people could only hope the gods would be favorable to them during life and the afterlife as a reward for good religious conduct.

Public Life Seen Through the Eyes of Tragedy

The relationship humans had with the gods further developed into artistic expression. The first tragedies were performed during an annual three-day-long festival dedicated to the god Dionysus. Although they had a religious connotation, some of these plays are still performed in theaters around the world. Comedy was of equal importance, and both comedies and tragedies reached their peak during the 5th century BCE. Just as in the Olympic Games, the drama festivities were competitive, and the writers were rewarded for the winning plays. Three tragedies and one comedy were chosen to be performed during the festival of Dionysus. The main stories tragedies told were the consequences humans had to endure for their malevolent interactions with the gods. After much bloodshed and suffering, a tragedy ended with a resolution to the trouble. The competition was also set for the best actor, and this is why, even today, the leading roles are called "protagonist," which means "first competitors."

Playwrights were usually men of the elite social class, but the actors and other performers were not. The playwrights not only wrote the tragedies but also composed the music, produced, directed, and often played as actors in their own plays. Some of the best classical Greece playwrights were Sophocles, Aeschylus, and Euripides. Their fame wasn't only due to their skills in drama. Aeschylus, for example, fought in the Battles of Marathon and Salamis. The rest held high offices and were elected as generals.

Aeschylus was praised for his military service, and the epitaph on his grave doesn't even mention his success as a playwright. But his own pride in his service to his homeland is expressed in his tragedies. Athenian tragedies were based on the writer's personal pride to be part of the greatest polis. Nevertheless, they often touched upon the ethical themes that sprouted between the humans and gods in the setting of the polis. This is because those themes turned out to be burning ethical questions at the time.

Some plays were mythological in character, and they seemingly took place in distant lands (Troy, for example). Nevertheless, the moral topics always illuminated society and the obligations of contemporary citizens in a polis. This is probably best displayed in Sophocles's play *Antigone*, with the conclusion that there is no easy resolution to the conflict between the divine moral traditions and the political rule of the state. Antigone, the protagonist, wants to bury her brother, who was proclaimed a traitor, while her uncle, the king, forbids it. The burial is a moral demand the humans owe to the gods. But the king needs to make a point about the treasonous act, so he denies the afterlife to him. The tragedy ends in the death of Antigone, as well as in the suicide of the king's wife and son. The king sees the suicide of his family as punishment of the gods, and he finally realizes the importance of tradition and burial rituals. Antigone was written nearly 2,500 years ago, but its moral message is relevant even for our times. The play is still produced in theaters around the world, though sometimes in a new modernized setting.

Many protagonists of Greek tragedies were female characters, although they were played by male actors. Women were not allowed to act, and they did not write plays. All characterizations of women were, therefore, left to the men. Heroines, such as Antigone, Clytemnestra, and Medea, are representations of what men thought Greek women were like. Perhaps the playwrights tried to give women a voice through their plays, but it seems this was not always true, mainly because ancient Greek women had strictly prescribed social behaviors and values, while the women who were the heroines of tragedies mainly spoke with a male voice. Although they were female in name and representation, they behaved and voiced their opinions as male citizens of Greek poleis. Only Medea perhaps represents a true woman. The play named after this heroine insists on a reevaluation of the role of women as wives and mothers. Medea keeps saying that women who bear children deserve the same respect as the hoplite warriors.

The audience and their reactions determined the popularity of plays. Women and men sat in the audience and were touched by the tragic messages the plays conveyed. But they were also greatly influenced by the issues raised by the plays, especially when it concerned gender relations, both in the family and in the polis. The Greek tragedy, just as its mythology, displays humans not as the ultimate villains but as common people susceptible to errors. They would fall out of divine favor due to moral mistakes they committed knowingly or even unknowingly. Thus, in a sense, the tragedies also served as warnings to the audience to mind their behavior at all times, or a similar fate could come upon them or on Athens itself. When the Greek tragedy was at its height, with audiences consuming the popular plays of Sophocles, Athens enjoyed immense power as it asserted full control over the Delian League. Through plays, the citizens were also reminded that the good fortune of Athens lay in the hands of the gods, and although the Athenians were the favorites of the divine, that could easily change.

Training and Education

Athenians didn't have a formal education in a modern sense, and public schools didn't exist. The norms of respectable behavior for both men and women were taught at home and through various events that occurred in their everyday lives. Private teachers existed, but only well-to-do families could afford them. Children's education consisted of learning how to write, read, and learn to play a musical instrument or to sing. For men, physical fitness was extremely important, and special attention was given to physical exercise. Military service demanded all men be in excellent form; after all, boys as young as eighteen and as old as sixty could be mobilized. This is why city-states provided men with open-air exercise facilities where they could work out on a daily basis. These facilities were named gymnasiums, which uses the ancient Greek term *gymnos*, which means "naked." Physical exercises were performed completely nude as both a tribute to the gods and as a promotion of male aesthetics. Some gymnasiums had a space dedicated to wrestling and boxing called a palaestra. But these spaces could exist independently, too, without being attached to gymnasiums. Other than spaces for exercising, gymnasiums also served as gathering spots where people could socialize, exchange political and intellectual ideas, or simply tell the news.

The daughters of wealthy men were given extensive education in writing, reading, and arithmetic, as they would need these skills to manage households successfully once they got married. Poor girls and boys had to learn some trade to help support their families. Usually, they learned the trade by helping their parents in their daily work. If they were fortunate enough, they could become apprentices to skilled craftsmen and artisans. The poor had little use of skills like reading and writing, and the general literacy rate in Athens was low. The poorest people knew only how to sign their names, but some individuals learned more than that. Communication was predominantly oral in classical Greece, and there was little reason for the commoners to learn how to read. If a legal dispute required them to read documents, they would simply find someone to read it to them.

The sons of prosperous families needed to acquire certain skills that would help them join the political life of Athens once they came of age. But there were no special schools that would prepare them for public life. Instead, they learned by observing their fathers, uncles, and other adult males. The most important skill a wealthy young man could acquire was the ability to persuade people during public speeches. Most older men would invite boys to be their students and would even have several such followers to teach. This form of education is today known as mentorship. The students were expected to help their mentors perform their daily duties in public office, but they were also their mentor's workout partners in gymnasiums. They were sometimes allowed to join drinking parties or symposiums where men exchanged political ideas. The relationship between a mentor and a student was often sexual; back then, though, it was seen as an expression of the bond that the pair shared and their dedication to each other.

For Greeks of the Classical period, it was normal for an older man to be attracted to both boys and girls. But that attraction was never seen as purely sexual. The relationship between lovers was more than just a desire; it was even seen as divinely inspired. But same-sex relations outside of the mentor-student relationship were frowned upon, and it brought disgrace to the people who practiced it. Even the relationships between mentor and student were heavily regulated. The older men were allowed to pursue their students, but the students were able to decline their proposals. Also, a mentor always needed to have a young man's education in mind, and one's sexual desire was to be satisfied only if it wouldn't influence the boy's education. Great Greek philosophers, such as Plato, believed that same-sex relationships between older men and young boys only helped society as a whole. That special bond was a motivating force behind one's education, values, and even war.

The overwhelming importance of persuasive speech resulted in the appearance of a new kind of teacher: the Sophists. They offered organized instruction to young men on how to develop public-speaking abilities. Their popularity grew immensely in the second half of the 5th century, but their popularity threatened to ruin the traditional relationship between mentors and students, and they were detested. Nevertheless, young men preferred Sophists because they were able to teach them precisely what they needed—the ability to persuade the masses or their opponents. Even those who failed to learn this oratory skill found ways to use the Sophists. They commissioned the Sophists and paid good money to have personalized speeches written especially for them. Then, they could present the speech as their own during public assemblies. The Sophists expected their pupils to pay for the classes, and unlike mentors, they didn't pursue sexual relationships. Wealthy young men flocked to the dazzling demonstrations these new teachers performed in public squares. But the teachings of many Sophists also brought new ideas to Athens, and many considered them dangerous to the city's political and social traditions.

Chapter 6: The Peloponnesian War

Battle of Syracuse
https://en.wikipedia.org/wiki/Peloponnesian_War#/media/File:
Destruction_of_the_Athenian_army_at_Syracuse.jpg

By the middle of the 5th century, the relations between Athens and Sparta had deteriorated greatly. Open hostilities erupted during the 430s, which means the peace signed in 445 failed to last the specified thirty years. The result was the Peloponnesian War (431-404 BCE), which engulfed most of the Greek world. This was one of the lengthiest ancient Greek conflicts, and it wreaked havoc on the social and political integrity of Athens, as it cut off its economic predominance and reduced its population. The war exposed the sharp division of the Athenian public, and the bitterness that ensued between political rivals brought a tragic end to some of the greatest individuals of the Classical period. The execution of the great Athenian philosopher Socrates proved that this political bitterness even survived the war.

The war itself was a result of Athens's stubbornness to negotiate a peace treaty. As the mightiest city-state, Athens believed it had the right to dictate the peace terms. However, what we know today about the Peloponnesian War comes mostly from the writings of Athenian historian Thucydides (460-400 BCE). He was a contemporary to the events, and he even served as a military general in the Athenian army. Eventually, he was exiled for the loss of one of Athens's outposts, and he took this time to interview and write down what other participants of the war had to say. His writing is analytical and direct, but it is impossible to say how much of the thoughts are his personal observations and exaggerations.

The Strategies of the War

The origin of the Peloponnesian War, like so many other wars, is complex. The immediate causes centered around the dispute between Sparta and Athens in the 430s. Athens wanted a free hand when dealing with Sparta's allies. However, the Spartans saw it as the Athenians trying to separate them from their allies. The first violent disputes occurred when Athens aided Corcyra, which was in conflict with Corinth (Sparta's greatest ally). At the same time, Athens militarily blocked Sparta's other ally, Potidaea. Megara, a former

Athens ally, rebelled, and seeking to break Athens's yolk, it sought help from Corinth. In return, Athens introduced the economic blockade of Megara, a city whose economy completely depended on seaborne trade. But underlying the immediate causes of the Peloponnesian War was the constant power play between Athens and Sparta. They feared each other's might and influence on the surrounding regions.

Sparta finally sent an ultimatum to Athens, but under the influence of Pericles, the Athenian assembly rejected it. In the ultimatum, the Spartans threatened war if the economic blockades of Megara and Potidaea weren't lifted. Corinth then put pressure on Sparta by threatening they would leave the Peloponnesian League if Sparta didn't react. Thus, it was the lesser powers that used their influence to nudge the two great city-states into a conflict.

Athens reminded Sparta of the obligations it had since it did sign a peace treaty in 445 BCE, but Sparta couldn't risk losing Corinth as an ally because it completely depended on its naval power, which could rival that of Athens. This is why the Spartans started blaming Athens for not even being willing to negotiate the terms and for refusing all concessions Sparta made after the ultimatum was rejected. Although the Spartans believed they were right, they still feared the punishment of the gods if they broke the peace treaty. Athens, on the other hand, was completely confident in achieving a victory in the ensuing war because they still considered themselves to be the gods' favorites; also, they were not the ones breaking the treaty.

Athens's urban center was safe from any direct attack due to the fortifications that surrounded it and the Athenian fleet resting in the harbor. After the Persian Wars, the Athenians encircled their polis with a high wall, leaving a fortified corridor that led to the main harbor at Piraeus. The technology of the mid-5th century wasn't sufficient enough to breach the walls of Athens. The result was a strongly defended city that had access to food supplies by importing grain from overseas. Even if the Spartans took all the agricultural land outside of

Athens's city walls, the citizens would not starve. Athens was rich, and it could always pay for food reserves by using the funds of the Delian League. Sparta was famous for its infantry and would surely attack from the land. Athens planned to send its fleet to attack Spartan territory by the sea or by landing its troops behind enemy lines. Pericles devised this two-pronged strategy to avoid open battle against the Spartan infantry in front of Athens's city walls. He was confident that Athens's wealth and manpower would be sufficient enough to win the war.

But the fault in Pericles's strategy was that it demanded many Athenians abandon their land and come to the urban center. Most Athenians lived in the countryside, and they proved to be unwilling to abandon their livelihood and move inside the city walls. The Spartans attacked Attica annually, and the people were required to move and abandon their everyday lives every so often. In 431 BCE, the first time Sparta attacked Attica during the war, the countryside-born and bred Athenians were forced to watch smoke rise from their destroyed homes and fields. They were angry, and Pericles had to do all that was in his power to stop the people from rushing outside to meet the Spartan infantry. The assembly wanted to ratify a new war strategy, but Pericles managed to persuade them to be patient. Unfortunately, Thucydides doesn't reveal how Pericles avoided the normal democratic procedures and blocked the assembly's meeting.

The Spartans spent one month ravaging Attica's countryside before they returned home. They didn't have the means to supply their army over a prolonged period, and they needed to rush home to avoid another helot uprising. Even though Sparta attacked Attica every year, the invasion never lasted more than forty days. Nevertheless, the Spartan army managed to inflict heavy losses on Athens and its countryside by burning and pillaging the whole region. Although the Athenians remained safe behind their walls and had enough supplies to last them through the war, they could not simply stand and watch the ravaging of their homeland.

The Unpredicted Disaster

Pericles's strategy was smart, and it produced results during the first years of the Peloponnesian War. However, an epidemic started ravaging the population of Athens in 430 BCE, and it took its greatest toll several years later. The consequences for Athens were disastrous. The polis was overpopulated with many people from the countryside. They stayed in cramped, narrow, and unsanitary dwellings, sharing them with the people who were already living in the urban center. Adequate housing and sanitation were missing, as the city leaders had failed to provide it for the people they invited to settle inside Athens. Pericles could only watch how his people disappeared. Thucydides described the symptoms of the disease, but modern scholars cannot determine what it was. The symptoms included painful sores, vomiting, diarrhea, and fever. Thucydides also describes how the disease made people extremely thirsty and how many of them jumped in water cisterns, contaminating the whole city's supply of drinking water. The mortality rate was so high that Athens had no power to man the fleet anymore. The failure of Pericles's strategy was imminent.

Pericles died of the same disease from which his people were suffering in 429 BCE, and the loss of his leadership damaged Athens the most. The Athenian confidence, a product of the belief that the gods favored them, started to wane. And so, the epidemic hurt Athens both physically and morally. The population was devastated, their political leader had been removed, and their self-confidence was crushed. The social and religious norms of the Athenians corroded since their faith in the divine was no longer important. But they continued their fight, and despite great losses, Athens's army managed to inflict damage on the Spartans. Potidaea was forced to surrender as early as 430 BCE, and in 429 BCE, the Athenian fleet won a major victory at Naupactus against Corinth. The city-states of Lesbos mounted a revolt, but the Athenians managed to suppress it in 427 BCE.

However, due to the division of the population started, many city-states in the Delian League started experiencing factional struggles. One such struggle led to a civil war in Corcyra in 427 BCE. The factional struggles in Athens prevented the Delian League from sending annual campaigns against Sparta in enough numbers for Pericles's strategy to work. The military campaigns of the early 420s brought horrible defeats to both sides, and it looked as if both Sparta and Athens were unable to gain the upper hand. But then, in 425 BCE, Athens's general, Cleon, captured 120 Spartan equals (citizens) and 170 infantry troops of the Peloponnesian League at Pylos, giving Athens a unique opportunity to press for peace.

In the previous history of Sparta, not a single man had ever surrendered. Their honor code wouldn't allow it. They preferred to die than to return home as losers. But at this point, the population of Spartan equals was extremely low, and it would be disastrous if the captured group perished. For the first time since the dawn of Sparta, the men chose to surrender. The Spartan leaders offered favorable peace terms to Athens in exchange for their equals. Cleon's victory brought him enormous popularity, and he used it to influence the Athenian assembly. He was a violent man, and he advocated a hard line toward Sparta. The Athenian assembly listened to his advice and refused the peace offer, believing they could win if they only continued fighting.

However, the next development in the war only served to prove that the Athenians lacked wisdom. The Spartans decided to abandon the traditional policy that prevented them from waging extended military expeditions outside of their territory. In 424, under the leadership of general Brasidas, the Spartan army embarked on a long campaign against Athens's many strongholds in the far north of Greece. They were hundreds of miles away from home, and there was no turning back. For Sparta, it was all or nothing. Such determination brought them their first major victory when they conquered Amphipolis, a colony essential to Athens's strategy. Amphipolis was

Athens's gateway to silver and gold mines, as well as to timber for shipbuilding. Although the contemporary historian Thucydides didn't fight in this battle, he was the commander of the region where Amphipolis was. The blame for the loss was put on him, and this was when he was exiled.

The Nonexistent Peace and the Sicilian Expedition

After the victory at Pylos in 425 BCE, Cleon became the most influential Athenian. He was dispatched to northern Greece in 422 to stop Spartan commander Brasidas. But both Cleon and Brasidas were killed before the Battle of Amphipolis, the battle the Spartan army won. Both Athens and Sparta had lost their most energetic military leaders, and their deaths opened the way to negotiations. Both sides decided to return to the power balance that was in place before 431, and the Peace of Nicias came in 421 BCE. The peace was named after an Athenian general, Nicias, who convinced the assembly to agree to the peace terms. Sparta signed the peace, but it caused a divide within the Peloponnesian League, as Corinth and Boeotia refused to sign it.

Factions appeared in both the Delian League and the Peloponnesian League that wanted to push the war and reach a decisive victory. The peace was unable to silence them. Among the Athenians was Alcibiades (450–404 BCE), who was one of the loudest people advocating against this uneasy peace. He was a member of the elite, and he was rich, brash, and fairly young. Alcibiades was also raised in Pericles's household after his father died (he was killed in a battle against the Spartans in 447), and this is probably what influenced his political views. Although he was young, he managed to gather a number of people who supported his advocacy against Spartan influence in the Peloponnese. In just a few years, Alcibiades started a new alliance made out of his Athenian followers, the like-minded people of Argos, and some of the city-states of the Peloponnese that were against Sparta. They believed that only through weakening Sparta could they achieve prosperity and political influence in the region. The geographical position of Argos was Sparta's biggest threat. Due to its location in the north of the Peloponnese, an attack launched from there could pin Sparta, rendering it out of options for a retreat. This is why the Spartans quickly raised their army and met the allied forces in the Battle of Mantinea in 418 BCE. They hoped for a quick victory that would eliminate the threat of Argos. However, the Peace of Nicias was still in effect, though it turned into a dead letter, as the violence started manifesting again.

In 416 BCE, Athens attacked Melos, an island city-state southeast of the Peloponnese. Melos was sympathetic toward Sparta, but it took no active part in the war against Athens, so it is unclear what Athens wanted to achieve with this aggression. Although greatly outnumbered, the inhabitants of Melos refused to surrender, hoping Athens would give up since the island was not a strategically important location, nor did it have some great treasure to be plundered. Once they were forced to surrender, the Athenians slaughtered all the Melos men and sold the women and children into slavery. Thucydides wrote about this conflict, but even he remains silent about the true motives behind Athens's attack. He puts the blame on Athens, describing its desire to dominate smaller poleis, and claims Melos only wanted to govern the relations between the states with justice. Thucydides described the conflict as a dialogue between the leaders of Melos and Athens (known as the Melian Dialogue), and it paints a perfect picture of the clash between ethics and power in international relations.

In 415 BCE, Alcibiades convinced the Athenian assembly to launch a campaign against Syracuse, an ally of Sparta. Syracuse might have been Sparta's political ally, but the main reason behind the attack was the fact that the island polis was very rich. But technically speaking, the Athenians attacked Syracuse only because another Sicilian city-state, Egesta (Segesta), was Athens's ally due to the treaty signed more than thirty years before. The Egestans supported Athens's willingness to conquer Syracuse, and they even encouraged it by falsely promising resources and military help that, in reality, they couldn't afford.

Before embarking with a fleet to Syracuse, Alcibiades was accused by his political enemies of taking part in the desecration of some Athenian monuments, as well as for mocking the Eleusinian Mysteries. He tried to have a trial while the army was still in Athens since he was popular among the soldiers. But his enemies managed to postpone the trial until the fleet was on its way to Sicily. Alcibiades went with the fleet, but a messenger was sent, demanding his immediate return to Athens alone. Instead of going back for the trial, Alcibiades defected to Sparta. The Athenian army lost a strong leader who could have kept motivating the army in the attack on Sicily. Nevertheless, they managed to win some initial victories due to the sheer size of the Athenian fleet. But their success was soon undermined by the indecisiveness of their leaders. To deal with the setbacks, the Athenian assembly decided to send reinforcements under the leadership of general Demosthenes. The new forces weren't enough. Athens failed to defeat Syracuse because, due to the persuasion of Alcibiades, Sparta sent help to its Sicilian ally. The decisive battle was fought in 413 BCE. The Athenian fleet became trapped in the Syracusan harbor and was ultimately crushed. Athens's only source of military might was completely destroyed.

The Final Ten Years of the War

Alcibiades's defection to Sparta continued to cause trouble for Athens even after the defeat in Sicily. Under his advice, Sparta established a permanent military base in Attica's countryside. They took advantage of Athens's weakness after the loss of its fleet at Syracuse to make a base of operations in Decelea, located in northeastern Athens. This was a perfect strategic position since Decelea overlooked the walls of Athens itself. The constant Spartan presence made working in the fields of Attica very dangerous, so Athens had to rely on food imported by the sea. This quickly drained the money reserves of the city-state, especially when twenty thousand slaves of Athens's silver mines escaped to Sparta. The flow of revenue from the mines came to a halt, forcing the government of Athens to change its policy. A new board of ten officials was installed to deal with the city's affairs. It was their task to supply the Council of 500.

After seeing Athens's misery that came due to the defeat in Sicily, Persia took an interest in Greek affairs once again. Persia quickly took control of western Anatolia and started financing a fleet to be used by Sparta and its allies. Some of the Ionian allies of the Delian League even took the opportunity to rebel against Athens. They were urged by Alcibiades, who was sent by the Spartans in 412 BCE to instigate unrest among the Ionian members of the Delian League. These riots disrupted the shipping lanes Athens used to import grain from Egypt and the shores of the Black Sea.

A great hardship started for Athens, but its citizens displayed only loyalty, devotion, and communal spirit when dealing with these problems. The excessive rebuilding of the fleet started immediately, and there was no lack of people willing to train how to serve on the ships. To finance the building of a new fleet, Athens had to tap into its emergency reserves that were stored at the Acropolis at the beginning of the Peloponnesian War. By 411, the Athenian naval force had been revived, and it successfully prevented the Corinthian fleet from sailing to Chios. It also managed to win some smaller battles along the coast of western Anatolia.

Despite these successes, political unity did not exist in Athens. Some influential individuals used the financial crisis to overthrow the democracy of the city-state and install a new oligarchic system. They insisted that the city should be led by a small group of elite-born individuals. Alcibiades made it known he would support such an oligarchic system in Athens and even acquire a Persian alliance for the city if democracy was removed. He hoped this would make it possible for him to return to Athens, but before he could persuade the Persian satraps of Anatolia to help him, the Spartans learned of his intentions. It didn't help that Alcibiades seduced the wife of one of Sparta's kings. In 411, the Athenian assembly turned the power over to a group of four hundred men in the hopes that a smaller governmental body would make wiser decisions and provide the city with better guidance in times of war. These four hundred men were tasked with electing the 500 who would represent Athens's main governmental body. In reality, the four hundred kept all the power of decision-making between themselves.

The four hundred elite men soon managed to destroy their unity because of power. Each one wanted to be the leader and assert his dominance over the others. The newly installed oligarchic system was doomed from the start, and it soon fell apart, as the Athenian fleet, which was stationed at the friendly city-state of Samos, threatened they would come back to Athens to reinstall democracy. The four hundred stepped aside but not before they invented a new system that mixed democracy and oligarchy. It was called the Constitution of the Five Thousand, and Thucydides praised it as the best form of government Athens ever had. The newly installed government then voted to recall Alcibiades and some other exiled military leaders in the hopes they could improve the Athenian army.

In 410 BCE, under the leadership of Alcibiades, the Athenian fleet won a great victory over Sparta at Cyzicus, a very important polis that controlled the connection of the trade routes between the Aegean Sea and the Black Sea. Despite the victory, the fleet continued to demand the full reinstalment of democracy in Athens, and the city leaders agreed to do so. However, this resulted in a return to the old politics, and when Sparta offered peace, Athens refused, just as before. Before dealing with Sparta's main base, the Athenian fleet went on to secure the grain routes and to persuade some of the defected members of the Delian League to return.

Sparta didn't offer peace because it could no longer fight. Instead, it wanted Athens to negotiate. At the time, a new leader arose in Sparta, the aggressive commander Lysander, who managed to doom Athens's hopes in winning the war by convincing Persia to finance the

Spartan fleet. The first defeat he inflicted on Athens came in 406 BCE at Notion near Ephesus. Alcibiades wasn't personally present, but he was deemed responsible for the loss, and he was forced into exile, this time never to return. Later that same year, Athens won a victory at the islands of Arginusae (south of Lesbos), but it also lost a great number of ships and men due to a storm. In a mass trial that followed, the fleet commanders were sentenced to death for their negligence. Sparta again sent a peace offer, and yet again, Athens refused. Lysander secured more Persian funds, and in 405, he decisively eliminated the Athenian fleet in the Battle of Aegospotami (Anatolia). To prevent Athens from recovering, he installed an economic blockade, forcing the city to surrender in 404 BCE. After twenty-seven years of war, Athens found itself at the mercy of Sparta.

The Corinthians demanded the total destruction of Athens since they were bitter enemies, but Sparta refused. Without the Athenian presence in Attica, the Corinthian fleet would be strong enough to block the access of trade ships to the Peloponnese. Instead, Sparta installed an anti-democratic regime in Athens known as the Thirty Tyrants. They were the members of the wealthy elite who had always despised democracy and favored oligarchy. They ruled for only eight months, but they terrorized the citizens by shamelessly stealing all the property they deemed to be desirable. It was common to see many wealthy men executed under false accusations just so the tyrants could take over his family possessions and valuables. They ruled so violently that even Sparta didn't react when pro-democracy individuals mounted a resistance and took over the city in 403 BCE. Athens once again had a functioning democratic government, but its financial and military powers were destroyed. The Athenian society continued to harbor the memories of the war and the defeat that had brought such bitter political divisiveness.

Athens after the War

The Peloponnesian War drained Athens's treasury and decimated its army. But it was the people who felt the most hardship after the war. Women who lost their husbands and male relatives in the war and who had no personal possessions were forced to seek work outside of Athens to survive. The worst situation was with the people who lived outside of Athens's urban center. They lost their homes to the Spartan attacks, and their fields were damaged. It would take some time before they were able to produce food again. The war forced many men and women to drastically change their way of making a living. The wealthy who had savings were the only ones safe from the economic crisis that followed the war. But most Athenians didn't have any valuables or money stored, and some of them even lost their businesses. The people couldn't afford to spend money, and many artisans and craftsmen had to close their shops. Those who were farmers had their livestock and harvest destroyed, and they had to search for work within the city as common laborers.

The wealthy women who lost their husbands had to completely start their lives over. They were used to weaving clothes at home and managing their households since the men earned money by serving in the army, farming, or engaging in trade. Without their husbands to provide for them, women had to accept low-paying jobs in vineyards or as wetnurses or weavers. More women joined the public life of Athens, although they were pushed there by the poverty caused by the war. However, no women's rights movement ever came to be, and women remained ousted from the political life of the polis.

Because Athens lost its silver mines due to the Spartan base at Decelea remaining in place, the city was no longer able to finance public building projects. Still, the will to carry on had to be maintained, and the city leaders continued investing in the building of the Erechtheum, a temple on the Acropolis. But other than that, the city funds had been drained in the attempt to revive its army, and many public events had to be canceled. To pay the war expenses, the city took the gold and silver items stored in Athens's temples, which they used to mint new coins. All citizens were required to exchange their silver and gold coins for cheaper ones made out of thin bronze.

The hardship of city life within Athens, both during and after the war, was somewhat elevated by the many comedies that were written and performed during this period. They were one of the main means of dramatic expression, together with tragedies. They, too, touched on current topics, but they also consisted of light humor, involving stories of bodily functions, sex, and imaginative profanity. However, the popular comedies were the ones that dealt with social issues. Aristophanes wrote one named *The Birds*. The protagonists of this comedy try to escape the poverty caused by the Peloponnesian War by leaving Athens for a new world called Cloud Cuckooland, which is inhabited by talking birds. Comedies in which women were portrayed as smart and witty were also popular. Through cleverly written dialogue, playwrights voiced female thoughts on the war, although they were written and performed by men. One of the most popular comedies that featured strong women was *Lysistrata*, written again by Aristophanes. In it, the heroine Lysistrata and other women of Athens refuse to have sex with their husbands to compel them to end the Peloponnesian War. They are even joined in this sex strike by the Spartan women. In the end, the sex, or lack of it, and the women's wits stop the gruesome war.

And so Athens entered the 4th century BCE in poverty and disgrace. But the end of the Peloponnesian War didn't mean the end of all conflict in Greece. Athens, Sparta, Thebes, Corinth, and many other city-states continued to fight for political dominance in the region. Fifty years after the Peloponnesian War, the poleis of ancient Greece still fought each other, but the only thing they achieved was to weaken each other. They created a power vacuum on an international scale, a void soon to be filled by the unexpected military and political rise of Macedonia, ruled by King Philip II (382–336 BCE).

Chapter 7: The Rise of Macedon

Philip II of Macedon
https://en.wikipedia.org/wiki/Philip_II_of_Macedon#/media/File:Phillip_II,_king_o
f_Macedonia,_Roman_copy_of_Greek_original,_Ny_Carlsberg_Glyptotek,_Copen
hagen_(36420294055).jpg

King Philip II had to reorganize his army to avoid an invasion from the north, but the changes he implemented gave him the power to extend his influence to the east and south, where Greek territory lay. In 338 BCE, at Chaeronea, he defeated the alliance of Greek city-states and formed the League of Corinth. He intended to use the combined Greek and Macedonian armies to start a vengeful war against Persia. Before he could do so, he was murdered, and his great kingdom was inherited by his son, the famous Alexander the Great (356-323 BCE), who followed in his father's footsteps and conquered the Persian Empire.

Alexander's conquests reached from Greece to the Near East, all the way to India. Although his wars were bloody and expensive, the result was a much better connection between Greece and the Near East, as well as the exchange of material goods and intellectual and cultural ideas. Alexander died unexpectedly before his son reached a mature age. He could not succeed Alexander as the king of Macedonia, and Alexander also didn't lay down a political arrangement for the conquered lands after his death. The new conditions of the late 4th century dictated events, and the structure of international power that Alexander had built collapsed.

Corinthian War (395-387)

Athens never recovered the might it once had in the 5th century. Even though the silver mine production started once again, it never produced at the same level as before. Nevertheless, the return of democracy did bring progress, and soon, Athens became a major power of the Greek world again. Sparta, on the other hand, tried to expand its influence immediately after the Peloponnesian War, but it only managed to provoke Athens and other Greek city-states. New diplomatic and military approaches were installed, and the first half of the 4th century BCE saw many shifting alliances. The weaker city-states would group together to resist the power play of the strong poleis, but the political disunity doomed those alliances, and they were short-lived.

In 401 BCE, Persian satrap Cyrus tried to unseat King Artaxerxes II of Persia (r. 404-358 BCE) with a mercenary army. It so happened that there were many Greek soldiers in Cyrus's army who supported his rebellion. They were disastrously defeated at Cunaxa near Babylon. The Spartans openly supported Cyrus, which enraged Artaxerxes. He was also provoked by the diplomatic and military efforts of King Agesilaus of Sparta and the Spartan commander Lysander, who tried to assert their control over western Anatolian regions and in northern Greece. Other prominent Spartan leaders meddled in the affairs of Greek poleis, and as a response to them, Sicily, Thebes, Athens, Corinth, and Argos allied. Persia offered its support to the alliance, and in 395, the Corinthian War started. Persia moved first.

In 397, Artaxerxes II started building a fleet, and he hired an Athenian named Konon (also spelled Conon) as its commander. The Spartans heard of the new Persian fleet, and they reacted by sending a large expedition against Persia in 396 under the leadership of King Agesilaus. He intended to establish a zone of rebel satraps in western Anatolia that would rise against Artaxerxes's rule, but the Spartans also helped Egypt keep its independence from Persia, which it managed to do until 340. The Greeks had an uneasy peace ever since the Peloponnesian War. Although Sparta asserted its dominance over Greece, it was never really safe, not even in its own territory of Laconia. The Spartans still struggled to control the helots, and the uprising of the slave-like helots recurred in 399.

Thebes was one of the most powerful enemies of Sparta. After the Peloponnesian War, Thebes emerged as a strong power, and it took control of Plataea in 427 BCE. Another reason for Thebes's power was that the federalization of Boeotia was reorganized after the war, allowing the Thebans to now control the federal magistrates. When Agesilaus prepared to leave for Anatolia, he wanted to perform a sacrifice ritual just like the legendary king Agamemnon did before the

Trojan War. However, he was stopped by the Boeotian magistrates, who were directly influenced by Thebes.

But Thebes didn't react this way for no reason. In fact, the city-state was reacting to the events in central Greece. There, Lysander was in command, and his actions threatened to encircle Thebes and Corinth, with the territories falling under Spartan influence. Sparta also interfered in the affairs of Corinth's colony of Syracuse, drawing even more anger toward itself. Unlike Thebes, Corinth didn't emerge as a powerful polis after the Peloponnesian War. Due to its weakness, Corinth agreed to merge itself with democratic Argos in a unique though short-lived political union. By 395 BCE, all of Sparta's enemies had a reason to start a war.

The opportunity to start the conflict presented itself when a quarrel between Locris and Phocis started. The Phocians appealed to Sparta to intervene, and Lysander responded by invading Boeotia. The Battle of Haliartus ensued, in which the Spartan general Lysander lost his life. That was a huge military loss for Sparta, which prompted Agesilaus to return from Asia and win two major battles against the allied enemies. His main opponent was Athenian general Iphicrates, who stationed his troops in Corinth. Although Agesilaus was victorious, he was unable to provoke the Athenians to accept an open battle.

At sea, the allies made more progress against Sparta. In August 394, Konon and Pharnabazus (the satrap of Phrygia) won the Battle of Cnidus in southern Anatolia. At this point, Sparta had to deal with another helot uprising back home, and a total victory was almost achieved by the allies. However, the violence continued for two more years. Finally, in 392, Sparta offered peace, abandoning its claims in Anatolia. But Artaxerxes was not ready to stop fighting. He couldn't forgive the Spartans for the support they gave to Cyrus. The war continued.

Although Persia and Athens were in an alliance against Sparta, in 392 BCE, under the leadership of Thrasybulus, the Athenians started their democratic institutions in the Anatolian cities. Persia finally realized that Athens was working against the interests of the empire, and it concluded a peace treaty with Sparta. With Persia's help, Sparta was able to block the Hellespont (Dardanelles), Athens's main trade route, starving Attica once again. Athens surrendered, and the peace was signed in 386 BCE, known as the King's Peace (or Peace of Antalcidas, who was the king of Sparta). It granted Cyprus and Clazomenae to Persia, but the majority of the Greek islands and city-states in the Aegean were given autonomy. However, Athens gained control over Lemnos, Imbros, and Scyros.

Any additional clauses to the peace remain unknown, and modern scholars still discuss various possibilities that could have been part of the treaty. However, they all agree that there was little change in Anatolia after the Corinthian War. Some evidence suggests that the Ionian cities remained autonomous after Sparta abandoned them. Anatolia as a whole became the political property of Persia, and this generalization was never seriously disrupted, even though the Greeks occasionally attacked. The political line dividing Greek and Persian interests became very clear after the King's Peace of 386, and it remained so even though many of the mercenaries Persia used were, in fact, Greek.

Philip II

The last decades of Artaxerxes's rule were marked by many uprisings in the western territories of the Persian Empire. They started as early as the 370s BCE when Datames, the governor of Cappadocia, proclaimed himself independent. By the middle of the decade, Hellespontine Phrygia had revolted with the joint help of Athens and Sparta. The last and greatest revolt was mounted in Mysia by its satrap Orontes. But at the same time, rebellions in Lydia and Caria began, each with different aims. All of these uprisings came to an end by the time of Artaxerxes's death in 359. They were not quelled by his army;

rather, they simply fell apart due to the rivalries between the rebel leaders. The successor to the Persian throne was Artaxerxes III, and he immediately ordered the dispersion of all the satraps' mercenary armies to prevent any possibility of future rebellions. This order was an early sign of the new vigor with which Persia was to be ruled.

At the same time, in Macedon, King Perdiccas III was killed in 359 or 360 in a battle against the Illyrians in the north. He was succeeded by his younger brother, Philip II, whose achievements would overshadow those of his predecessors. But Philip's achievements would later be diminished by the successes of his son, Alexander the Great. This is why there is a lack of evidence for Philip's early rule and the consolidation of power. As tradition explains, the Macedonians inhabited the region of Macedonia or Macedon (today's northern Greece and North Macedonia) after migrating from the area known as Thessalian Perrhaibia and from the regions surrounding Mount Olympus. They brought their Greek religion with them, although local variations sprouted. The language of Macedon was Greek in its base, and all of the personal names are of Greek origin. But this cultural Hellenization is strongly contradicted by the social and military structure of Macedon. Instead of resembling the Greeks, it strongly resembled the structures of later European feudal societies. The Macedonian kings of the 4th century BCE granted land in exchange for military service, and this system was similar to the one present in Persia.

King Philip II was known for his preference for diplomacy rather than military intervention. When dealing with his enemies, he always tried to calm the situation first, if only to buy some time and prepare his armies. In his early years on the throne, he had to deal with the Illyrians and Thracians, who saw the opportunity to invade Macedonia upon the death of Philip's older brother, Perdiccas. But Philip managed to thwart this invasion by promising his enemies a yearly tribute. In reality, he was buying time to prepare his army for a greater conquest. Philip wanted to expand his kingdom and take over parts of central Greece. Sparta was busy trying to conquer Messenia, Persia was fighting its wars in Egypt, and Thebes diluted its power by overextending. The only serious threat would come from Athens, but Athens relied on its fleet to attack, and Philip was aware that Macedon couldn't be approached by the sea during a certain time of the year due to the etesian winds of the Aegean Basin. He needed to perfectly time his invasion of central Greece. Thasos controlled the silver mines of the Pangaion region, but it had no military power to defend them, and Philip was certain he could easily deal with Thasos.

To reorganize his army, Philip introduced extensive training and started hiring mercenaries. He tested his new army against the Illyrians and other northern enemies, and he was victorious, expanding his territory to the north as far as Lake Ohrid. In 358, he visited Thessaly to prepare an attack on Amphipolis, which was launched the next year. He kept Athens away from meddling by promising he would give Amphipolis to them, but he never did. Instead, he continued his conquest and took Pydna and Crenides, mining cities. The Olynthians became alarmed by Philip's conquest, and they rushed to ally with him. Philip accepted it, as he preferred diplomacy over war. Athens tried to stop Philip when he launched a conquest of Thrace, but it didn't have much success. At the time, Athens had troubles of its own with the outbreak of the Social War in 357, which led to the break of the Second Athenian League, which included the great poleis of Chios, Byzantium, and Methymna. But the war went badly for Athens, and in 355, it had to accept a very disadvantageous peace because Artaxerxes III threatened a Persian intervention.

In Thessaly, Philip used his diplomatic skills to convince the Greek leaders to install him as the commander of the armies of the Thessalian League. With this, he became the leader of Greece, as, at that moment, Thessaly was one of the most prosperous regions. Macedonia was never part of Thessaly, but it was its neighbor, just over the mountains of southern Macedonia. Since Philip claimed that the great Greek hero Heracles was his ancestor, the Thessaly leaders saw him as their kin. In their eyes, he was perfectly qualified to become a Greek leader. But in reality, the league needed the king of Macedon to form an alliance with Thebes and to defeat a tyrant that ruled in Thessaly. It took two defeats before Philip was able to expel the tyrant Lycophron, but the league was amazed by his success and named him the leader of their armies.

Due to the alliance between Thebes and the Thessalian League, Philip II became involved in the Third Sacred War (355-346 BCE), helping Thebes to take Phocis. Athens was an ally of Phocis, which was the cause of the eruption of hostilities between Macedon and Athens. However, Philip was defeated by the Phocians, something nobody could have predicted. But Philip managed to recover by 352, and he reversed the defeat at the Battle of Crocus Field. This victory brought Philip enormous prestige, which he used to take over the leadership of Thessaly in a fuller sense. He acquired its ports, trade, and mine revenues, which he used at his will. Southern Thessaly was also a gateway to central Greece, and at the end of 352, Philip tried to invade using the same pass of Thermopylae the Persians had previously tried to use to enter the Greek mainland. Athens stood up to defend it. Philip then laid a siege on Heraeum Teichos (in Thrace) in 351, prompting Athenian statesmen Demosthenes to denounce Macedonian imperialism and promise Athens would move to counter Philip. But it was too late, and Athens couldn't do much in defending Thrace.

The conflict between Athens and Macedonia continued in 349 when Philip decided to attack Olynthus, even though they had been in alliance since 356. Olynthus asked Athens for help, and even though Athens responded, the city fell in 348. Its citizens were sold into slavery, and their poor treatment prompted Euboea to revolt, as Athens proved incapable of protecting its allies. By the end of the 340s, King Philip II managed to unite the northern and significant parts of central Greece and impose his international plans on them.

He was preparing to launch the conquest of the Persian Empire, but he was aware of the Persian might. He knew that he needed to add the army of southern Greece to his own to be able to launch his grandiose invasion.

However, Athens continued to resist him. In 338, Athens and Thebes entered a coalition, intending to block Philip's plans and military actions. That same year, they fought the Battle of Chaeronea in Boeotia, in which Philip defeated the Athens-Thebes coalition. The peace they signed stated that the defeated Greek city-states would keep their independence as long as they joined Philip's alliance. Modern scholars call this alliance the League of Corinth, although Corinth as a polis lost its influence in Greece a long time ago.

The Battle of Chaeronea marks the beginning of a period in which Greek city-states stopped making foreign political decisions for themselves and followed a stronger, outside power. They were no longer independent to make foreign policies, but they continued to be the backbone of Greek economic and social structures. Throughout the reign of Philip, his son Alexander, and the Hellenistic kingdoms that followed the death of Alexander the Great, Greek city-states remained an important factor, as the great new monarchs needed their loyalty and the taxes they paid. The many poleis of Greece continued to be an important political element of the ancient world, but they would never again be independent entities completely able to guide their destiny.

Back home, in Macedonia, some individuals didn't understand Philip's motives in creating the Corinthian League. They preferred straightforward conquest that would allow them to loot rich Greek city-states such as Thebes or Athens. To appease his people and to consolidate his power, Philip depicted himself as the thirteenth god of Olympus. He would never risk showing the Greeks such representations of himself, but in Macedonia, he thought it would install fear and respect. He might have even received a cult in Philippi, previously known as Crenides; it was renamed to Philippi after it fell to Philip's army. However, it is not known if he was worshiped as a god anywhere else in Macedonia. Scholars believe he had no time to spread his cult through the lands he ruled because he was suddenly assassinated in 336. The perpetrator remains unknown and so do his motives.

Chapter 8: Alexander the Great

Roman bust of Alexander the Great
https://en.wikipedia.org/wiki/Alexander_the_Great#/media/File:Alexander_the_Great,_from_Alexandria,_Egypt,_3rd_cent._BCE,_Ny_Carlsberg_Glyptotek,_Copenhagen_(5)_(36375553176).jpg

Philip II was in the prime of his life when he was assassinated. His successor, Alexander III of Macedon (better known now as Alexander the Great), reacted swiftly and with a cool head to his father's death. Many contemporaries and modern historians believe that Alexander was actually behind his father's assassination. Some believed Philip was killed by Olympias, his wife and the mother of his successor. Nevertheless, the young prince quickly arrested and killed the highly suspected individuals, most of whom were his rivals. Then again, Alexander's succession was never in question since he was Philip's oldest legitimate son. He also enjoyed the support of the people compared to the son of Philip's predecessor, who was still alive at the time and was a possible pretender to the throne.

Alexander was barely twenty years old when he became the king of Macedonia. Although his succession was smooth, he was forced to deal with Macedonia's northern enemies as soon as he came to the throne. Their traditional enemies, the Illyrians and Thracians, thought to use Philip's death to break free of Macedonian dominion. But in a couple of swift campaigns, Alexander was able to subdue them without any losses of territory or his army. Alexander then took the opportunity to conquer even more territory in the north, and the expeditions there led him across the Danube. In the meantime, the Thebans believed Alexander had been killed somewhere in Illyria, and they tried to break off from the Corinthian League. It took Alexander only seven days to reach Thessaly and five more to enter Boeotia. He not only subdued Thebes but also destroyed the city as an example to all the other Greek poleis that considered abandoning the league.

Alexander in Anatolia and Egypt

With the succession of the Macedonian throne, Alexander also succeeded the leadership of the Persian conquest. Once he dealt with the rebellious city-states, he started the campaign in Asia, doing so in 334. He installed his general Antipater as the governor of Greece, leaving 12,000 infantry and 1,500 cavalry units in his charge.

Alexander took forty thousand foot soldiers and over six thousand cavalrymen with him to Asia. He had inherited this army, as well as the plans of the conquest, from his father, and it remains unknown if he had to make any changes and reorganize the army before he launched the campaign. But as time passed, and during the conquest itself, he often changed plans, adapting them to new circumstances. He also rethought the supply of his army and started using wagons to haul equipment and provisions. This was his addition to his father's army, as Philip's soldiers had to carry their weapons, armor, and provisions.

The core of Alexander's infantry was the Macedonian phalanx, a rectangular military formation in which the soldiers stood very close to each other to make an impregnable wall. They were armed with long spears or any kind of long weapon, which they used to keep the enemy at a distance. The main body of the cavalry was called the Companions, which was led by Alexander himself, positioned on the head of the right wing. The left one was led by Philip's favorite general, Parmenio, the commander of the Thessalian part of the cavalry. The army also had additional troops such as scouts, slingers, and other irregulars. They all had light armor and any weapons they could muster. Alexander also made use of war machines, such as siege engines, that could be easily assembled on the spot. They were cared for by the Thessalian siege engineers previously employed by Philip. These machines were probably the reason for his swift victories in Anatolia. When Alexander crossed the Hellespont with his army, he threw his spear into the ground and laid claim to the whole of Asia. First, he visited Troy, where he paid his respect to the heroes of old, Ajax and Achilles.

Artaxerxes III died in 338, leaving behind a power vacuum. His death also made the conquest of Asia (in a sense, the Persian Empire) much easier than it had been during his life and those of his predecessors. The next in line was Darius III, a much weaker king, who assumed the throne only in 336. Darius managed to convince the

Anatolian satraps to gather an army and oppose Alexander's conquest. The first conflict occurred in the general region of Xanthus (in modern-day Turkey), and the combined Greco-Macedonian army found itself facing a large Persian force. This was not the main Persian army, but it was sizable, and the conflict was bloody. Alexander the Great won, though, opting for a daylight battle and the personal leadership of his cavalry. If anything, Alexander contributed to history with his heroic generalship, as he would always personally lead his army and shout a battle cry dedicated to the Greek gods. After the battle, Alexander immediately reorganized the satraps in Anatolia, giving leadership to his own men. In a sense, he declared that he wouldn't change the organization of the Persian Empire. He only planned to succeed it. However, he did install democracy, restored the laws, and ended the tradition of the Ionian cities of sending tribute to the Persian king.

Alexander proved to be very rewarding toward the Ionian city-states that rebelled against the Persians during his father's rule. For instance, on the island city-state of Chios, Alexander left a monument to testify to the beginning of democracy. Many cities bear his name, but it is unknown if he founded them or merely renamed them. He certainly rebuilt the poleis that had been destroyed during combat. One such example is Priene, a very old city of Ionia. The city was crumbling, and it is unknown if Alexander renewed it with building projects or if he re-founded it, bringing new people to settle in the place where old Priene used to be. Whatever was the case, the city was physically reconstructed during Alexander's time, and so were many other Anatolian Greek cities, e.g., Heraclea and Smyrna.

The next encounter with the Persians was in 334 BCE at Halicarnassus, and this was where Alexander met the strongest resistance. The Persians brought their fleet to the city in order to make a new defense line. However, the political events before Alexander's conquest determined Halicarnassus's fate. Its former queen, Ada of Caria, was overthrown by her brother. He soon died, and Darius III installed a Persian satrap to rule Caria. Alexander met Ada at the fortress of Alinda, which was still in her possession, and the two developed a mother-son relationship. She used her influence to get Alexander's army near the city, and after some fighting, the city fell. However, the retreating Persians burned it, leaving only ruins for Alexander and Ada. Nevertheless, Ada was restored as the rightful queen of Caria, and in turn, she officially adopted Alexander as her son.

After Halicarnassus, in 333 BCE, Alexander moved his army to the east. In the Battle of Issus, he had the first opportunity to meet Darius III, who came to personally lead his army. Alexander used his characteristically bold tactic of leading his cavalry in the attack on the right side of the Persian lines. A flanking maneuver against Darius's position, who was in the center of his army, followed, and the Persian king was forced to flee for his life. By tradition, Darius was accompanied by his wives and daughters, and he decided to leave them behind while he escaped. Alexander's chivalrous treatment of the captured Persian royal women became legendary. But at the time, it served to boost his support among the local people of Anatolia.

In 332 BCE, Tyre, a city on the coast of Lebanon, refused to surrender, forcing Alexander to use the siege engines he inherited from his father. The walls of Tyre cracked, and the city fell after a lengthy siege, losing its reputation of being an impregnable city (this was the first time in its history that it had fallen). However, the siege engines weren't typically successful. It was still almost impossible to wreck the walls of fortified cities, and it seems that Tyre was just luck. Nevertheless, the citizens of walled Anatolian cities never again felt safe behind their defenses. The unity of the people often broke under the psychological pressure they felt when they saw the siege engines and catapults.

With the conquest of Anatolia finished, Alexander turned toward Egypt, which he took without a struggle. Archaeologists found hieroglyphic inscriptions that seem to describe how Alexander presented himself as the successor to the Persian Empire. In 331, he founded Alexandria, a city on the west shore of the Nile River. This was the first of many cities we know for sure was founded by Alexander. Alexandria was founded by the joining of several villages, but the main intention of Alexander the Great was to Hellenize Egypt through public building projects. He also introduced Greek-style athletic games and tragic and comedic plays. During his time in Egypt, Alexander visited the oracle of Ammon, a counterpart of the Greek Zeus. The oracle was settled far in the western Egyptian desert in the oasis of Siwah (Siwa). Alexander never revealed what was told to him by the oracle. However, the news got out that he was told that he was the son of a god and that he accepted it as the truth.

From Egypt, Alexander crossed Phoenicia. In the open field of Gaugamela (northern Mesopotamia), he met Darius III once more. The battle started in October 331 BCE, and Alexander managed to crush the king's army and proclaim himself the king of Asia. The Persian Empire was extremely heterogeneous, and the fact that the new king was Macedonia did not alarm them. There was no change to the lives of the empire's population anyway. They continued to pay taxes, sending them to a distant king they would never know or see. As in Egypt, the local Persian administrative system was left in place, but only some of the Persian governors were replaced with Macedonians and Greeks. This was probably done because Alexander had a long-term plan to make the Macedonians, Greeks, and Persians work together for them all to assimilate into one single empire under his rule.

To India and the Death of Alexander

Conquering the Persian Empire wasn't enough for Alexander's megalomaniac personality. He decided to lead his army eastward, probably in search of the farthest point and the edge of the world, although Aristotle, his teacher from his younger days, believed the earth was round. But going east, through lands the Macedonians and Greeks had never even heard of, meant many hardships had to be overcome. The supply of the army was the biggest problem, as the land they passed was arid. Hoplites were used to carrying their own provisions but never for this long and this far away from home. The army marching through the hostile lands was also followed by a large number of non-combatants, such as entertainers, merchants, wives and children of soldiers, and prostitutes. The army commanders weren't responsible for feeding the non-combatants, but their numbers meant less food could be foraged or hunted for the soldiers. The merchants would go in front of the army and buy whatever they could from the locals, only to sell it to the army's provisional officers at much higher prices. The local population consisted of farmers, but they often had no surplus to sell.

Since Alexander marched his army through what he considered to be friendly land, he expected the locals to provide for his soldiers. They needed to donate the food for the passing army or to sell it for money, which they had no use for. The remote villages sustained themselves, and they had nowhere to go to buy the food they now lacked. Starvation often came after Alexander's Greco-Macedonian army passed by.

In 329, from the heartland of Persia, Alexander marched his army toward the steppes of Bactria and Sogdiana (in modern-day Afghanistan and Uzbekistan). There, he fought highly mobile locals, but he was unable to defeat them. His army was used to open battlefields, while the locals preferred guerilla-style tactics. In the end, Alexander satisfied himself by negotiating an alliance with the local tribes. The alliance was sealed with the marriage of Alexander and a local princess named Roxane (Roxana) in 327 BCE. Alexander took the opportunity of peace to deal with his opposition. Those who resisted his plans to keep going east were accused of treachery and disloyalty, and they were executed on the spot. Among them were some of the leading commanders of Alexander's army. Alexander was known for using terror to discourage rebellions.

From Bactria, Alexander pushed his armies through monsoon rains for seventy days toward India. The soldiers' resolution finally shattered, and in the spring of 326 BCE, they raised a mutiny against Alexander, even though the army had just achieved a great victory against King Porus in what is today Punjab. Alexander wanted to proceed toward the Bengal region, and his soldiers were not in the mood to face another great army. They had already been away from home for so long, something that Macedonian and Greek armies had never practiced before. All of the expeditions were kept short so that the soldiers could go back home and contribute to the public and political life of their poleis. Whenever his troops showed a lack of morale, Alexander was always able to inspire them or at least shame them into action. But this time, he could do nothing to persuade them to proceed, and he had to agree to take them home. However, he wouldn't allow them a simple march home. Instead, he ordered attacks on local tribes who resisted accepting his dominance. Alexander personally fought, often risking his life. Perhaps he did it to inspire his troops, but more often than not, he horrified his generals, who had to save him on a couple of occasions. Once, he climbed the walls of a town practically alone and was dangerously wounded before his troops were able to rescue him.

Once he reached the mouth of the Indus River, Alexander decided to divide his army in three. One part of his army was sent on the eastern route inland. Under the command of general Craterus, the largest portion of the army marched to Carmania (today in Iran). Alexander sent the second part of the army, under the leadership of admiral Nearchus, westward along the coast of the Persian Gulf to explore possible spots for founding new cities. Alexander personally led the last part of his army toward Persia through the dangerous deserts of Gedrosia and Makran. He planned to surpass the prestige of previous Persian kings by achieving what they considered to be impossible; marching through the desert. Most of the non-combatants who followed the army were lost, but hunger, thirst, and exhaustion also took the lives of many soldiers. In the Gedrosian desert, scientists frequently measure temperatures up to 127°F (52.7°C) in the shade. Alexander shared the hardships with his men, and it is said he often refused water, choosing to suffer just like his army did. Finally, they reached safety in Susa, in the Persian heartland, in 324 BCE.

Alexander wasn't finished with the war, and upon his arrival in Susa, he immediately started planning an invasion of the Arabian Peninsula, which he would then follow up with the North African territories west of Egypt. By the time he was back from his Indian campaign, Alexander had stopped pretending he ruled Greece as anything less than an absolute monarch. Earlier, he promised internal freedom to loyal Greek cities, but he sent a decree in which he demanded they restore citizenship to all who were exiled before. He did so because the increased number of exiled influential men created tension in the Greek world. These men belonged nowhere, but they still asserted political influence, turning cities against each other. Alexander also demanded some Greek cities recognize his divinity, and the poleis sent delegations to honor him as one of the Olympian gods. Previously, many modern scholars believed Alexander wished divinity because the city-states would be obliged to follow all of his commands, as they would be the commands of a god. But this theory is considered wrong, as it seems that he convinced himself that he was actually Zeus's son. Because of his successful conquests of the known world, Alexander also believed he surpassed the deeds of many famous Greek heroes and that he was no longer merely a mortal. In ancient terms, Alexander's divinity emerged as a consequence of his power, and it was natural and righteous.

Alexander's conquests benefited humankind on many levels. He united the known world into a single political entity, but he also allowed many geographical units to stay administratively independent. He also recognized the experience local leaders had, and he didn't always replace them with Greek generals. The new cities Alexander founded along the way served as royal outposts that made sure the whole region would stay loyal to him. They also served to open new trade possibilities between the regions, making the exchange of goods and ideas easier. He pushed for not only conquest but also exploration, and he would always have scientifically minded individuals with him. His explorations revealed more information on geography, botany, mathematics, and medicine to Greek scholars, who later passed their knowledge to the Western world.

Alexander's plans to conquest Arabia and North Africa ended with his premature death. The great conqueror and leader died on June 10th, 323 BCE, in Babylon. He was only thirty-two years old, and there are two different accounts of his death. Plutarch, a Greek philosopher and historian, claimed Alexander entertained his generals and spent day and night drinking with his friends. This caused him to develop a fever that lasted for fourteen days, rendering him incapable of speech until he finally died. Diodorus, another ancient Greek historian, wrote that Alexander experienced a sudden great pain after he drank undiluted wine. He was very ill for the next eleven days, after which he died. According to Diodorus, there was never any fever. But many contemporary historians seem to agree that foul play was involved in Alexander's death. In ancient times, poisoning was a common way of getting rid of one's political enemies. Only Plutarch dismissed the theory of poisoning, but modern historians still can't agree on what was the real cause of Alexander's death. Some suggest that poison with such a long action wasn't known in antiquity. After all, Alexander the Great died between eleven and fourteen days after he initially got sick. Some propose he contracted typhoid fever or malaria and that he died due to illness, not poison.

Alexander had made no plans about what should be done with his great empire after his death. He had no children yet, although his wife Roxane was pregnant at the time of his death and would give birth several months later. Alexander's closest friends asked him on his deathbed about who should inherit his kingdom. He only answered, "to the most powerful" (Arrian, Anabasis of Alexander 7.26.3). But since some ancient writers claimed Alexander lost the ability to speak during his illness, this story may be apocryphal.

The plan was to take Alexander's body back to Macedon for burial, but Ptolemy II of Egypt confiscated the sarcophagus with his remains and took it to Alexandria, where it remained until the end of antiquity. But its later fate is unknown, and it remains yet to be discovered.

Because Alexander had no successor, his vast empire was ravaged by the succession war. Finally, it was divided into four: Ptolemaic Egypt, Antigonid Macedon, Attalid Anatolia, and the Seleucid Empire, which controlled Mesopotamia and Central Asia.

Conclusion

Nineteenth-century scholars invented the term Hellenistic to mark the period that started with the death of Alexander the Great in 323 BCE. The break-up of his vast empire meant many political, cultural, and social changes, not only in Greece but also throughout the whole known world. The earliest Hellenistic period saw the emergence of new kingdoms and a new form of kingship, as Alexander's successors were his generals who had no blood relations to any of the royal families that previously existed. They also didn't have a historical claim to the land they governed, yet they were accepted as the successors of the great leader. Still, acceptance didn't come easily. It was forced by military power, prestige, and the ambition of Alexander's generals-turned-monarchs.

The end of Alexander's Persian Empire thus came at the same time as the end of the Classical period. The beginning of the Classical period began with Greece recognizing Persia as its national enemy, a Greece that never could have comprehended being a part of Persia, let alone being the driving force behind that unity. The unity of the ancient Greeks had started with recognizing Persia as their enemy, with Sparta, the strongest polis, being the original leader. But for a variety of reasons, Sparta could no longer continue the war against Persia, and the leadership of the struggle passed to Athens and the

Delian League. The conflict continued until 449 BCE, and Athens managed to drive Persia away from Ionia and the western Anatolian coast.

With no enemy to fight, the Delian League transformed into the Athenian empire, in which many Greek city-states became subordinate to Athens. In turn, Athens became the richest and most powerful political entity in Greece, and although it promoted democracy in itself, it discovered how easy it was to oppress other poleis. But even Athens's democracy was designed so it could exclude certain people. Women, foreigners, slaves, and those who could not prove their Athenian lineage could not make any state decisions. Citizenship was a privilege only for those who could prove both his parents were born Athenians. But soon, it became obvious that not everyone agreed with the democracy in the Greek world, as some still preferred the oligarchy. So, a conflict between Athens, a champion of democracy, and Sparta, a champion of the oligarchy, began, a conflict known as the Peloponnesian War. Athens had the advantage of being the economic and intellectual center of Greece. In this period of uncertainty and war, some of the best art was produced in Athens in the form of both architecture and literature.

The Peloponnesian War came to a halt with the Thirty Years' Peace in 445, but many revolts in Athens reversed its role as the economic center. The conflict resumed in 431 when the balance of power between Athens and Sparta was overturned. Athens's ambitions became far too great and unchecked, and the polis provoked Sparta into another war. In 404, the fighting was over, thanks to Persia meddling in Greek affairs. It sided with Sparta and helped bring Athens to its knees.

But soon, a new conflict arose, this time between Sparta and Persia when Sparta saw fit to liberate Greek cities in Anatolia from Persian rule. The new war is remembered as the Corinthian War, and this time Athens joined the Persian side. The end came in 386 with the King's Peace or Peace of Antalcidas. Sparta agreed to leave the

Anatolian Greek cities as Persian possessions but proclaimed all other Greek cities and islands as autonomous.

However, Sparta couldn't forget about Ionia, and it proceeded to interpret the peace treaty as it saw fit. The Spartans escalated the situation with their attempt to occupy Thebes, and Athens responded to the aggression by starting the Second Athenian League to fight Spartan imperialistic tendencies. Many alliances were switched during this period, and in the mainland conflict, Athens saw fit to help Sparta against Thebes when Thebes started grabbing power for itself.

While the Greek poleis quarreled over dominance, in the far north, Macedon was on the rise. Shielded by a mountain range and the unpredictable waters of the Aegean Sea, Macedon started looking at southern Greece as a possible source of revenues. But the intentions to exploit the south turned into an ambition to unite the whole of Greece when Macedon's King Philip II came to rule. Philip was able to exploit the sentiment of Persia being a national enemy to gain full control over Greece. He even started planning a conquest of Persia as retaliation for all the evils it had committed upon Greece, but he was assassinated before any action was taken.

His son and successor, Alexander the Great, took his father's dream upon himself. The great leader that he was, he not only conquered Persia but also went on to further explore the east, intending to reach the end of the world, which was, in his mind, just east of India. Instead of discovering the world's edge, Alexander brought the end of the Classical period by failing to name a successor before his untimely death. But the world didn't end with Alexander the Great, as many contemporaries certainly believed. It continued into a new era, one that brought the foundation of many Greek cities in Asia with Greek and Macedonian rulers. This new period lasted through the rise of Rome until, finally, Rome became powerful enough to dare venture and take over the Hellenistic world.

Here's another book by Captivating History that you might like

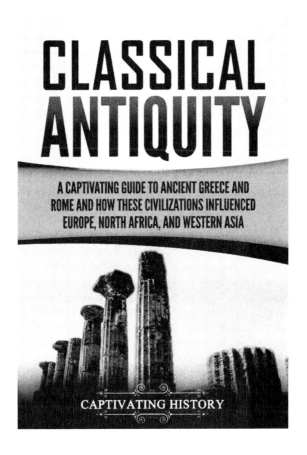

Free Bonus from Captivating History (Available for a Limited time)

Hi History Lovers!

Now you have a chance to join our exclusive history list so you can get your first history ebook for free as well as discounts and a potential to get more history books for free! Simply visit the link below to join.

Captivatinghistory.com/ebook

Also, make sure to follow us on Facebook, Twitter and Youtube by searching for Captivating History.

References

Bury, J. B. (2015). *A History of Greece: To the Death of Alexander the Great*. Cambridge: Cambridge University Press.

Cartledge, P. (2016). *Sparta and Lakonia: A Regional History 1300-362 BC*. Place of publication not identified: Routledge.

Everitt, A. (2017). *Rise of Athens: The Story of the World's Greatest Civilization*. New York: Random House.

Grote, G. (2008). *History of Greece: From the Earliest Period to the Close of the Generation Contemporary with Alexander the Great*. Place of publication not identified: Hesperides Press.

Henderson, B. W. (1973). *The Great War between Athens and Sparta: A Companion to the Military History of Thucydides*. New York, Arno Press.

Herodotus, Godley, A. D., Herodotus, & Herodotus. (2004). *The Persian Wars*. Cambridge, MA: Harvard University Press.

Martin, T. R. (1996). *Ancient Greece: From Prehistoric to Hellenistic Times*. New Haven: Yale University Press.

Osborne, R. (2000). *Classical Greece: 500-323 BC*. Oxford: Oxford University Press.

Pickard-Cambridge, A. W., Gould, J., & Lewis, D. M. (2003). *The Dramatic Festivals of Athens*. Oxford: Clarendon Press.

Robinson, C. A., & Greenberg, L. (1984). *Ancient Greece*. New York: F. Watts.

Starr, C. G. (1991). *A History of the Ancient World*. New York: Oxford University Press.

Thucydides, Hammond, M., & Rhodes, P. J. (2009). *The Peloponnesian War*. Oxford: Oxford University Press.